DREAMLAND'S

GRADED
MATHEMATICS

PART - 2

By
SUSHMA NAYAR
M.Sc. I (D.U.), B. Ed.
H.O.D Mathematics
Delhi Public School,
Mathura Road, New Delhi-3

Published by

DREAMLAND PUBLICATIONS

J-128, KIRTI NAGAR, NEW DELHI - 110 015, (INDIA)
Fax : 011-2543 8283 Tel : 011-2510 6050
E-mail : dreamland@vsnl.com
www.dreamlandpublications.com

Published in 2010 by
DREAMLAND PUBLICATIONS
J-128, Kirti Nagar, New Delhi - 110 015 (India)
Tel : 011-2510 6050, Fax : 011-2543 8283
E-mail : dreamland@vsnl.com
www.dreamlandpublications.com

ISBN 81-7301-259-8
Printed at : **Shalini Offset Press**

Preface

Graded Mathematics is a series of nine books—Parts 0 to 8—meant for children of KG to class VIII. The series is a beautiful blend of the text and the pictures. It is a class by itself as far as the subject of Mathematics is concerned.

The topics in each book are in conformity with the latest syllabus issued by the NCERT. They have been pictorially graded in such a manner as to suit the needs of the concerned age-group. The children have been introduced to each topic through pictures so that they may grasp the topic without much difficulty.

There are a host of black-and-white designed books on Mathematics flooding the market. But the books of our series are off the beaten track. As far as the designing in our books is concerned it is in line with international standards.

We are glad to place this unique series in the hands of the teachers and the taught with a hope that it will admirably meet their approval from every angle. Constructive suggestions for the betterment of the series are highly welcome.

— AUTHOR

Contents

1 WHAT WE HAVE LEARNT

Count, **write** and then **add**.

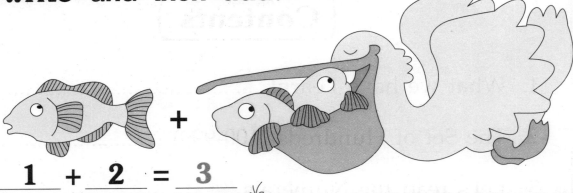

$$\underline{\hspace{1em}1} + \underline{\hspace{1em}2} = \underline{\hspace{1em}3}$$

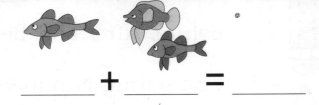

$$\underline{\hspace{3em}} + \underline{\hspace{3em}} = \underline{\hspace{3em}}$$

$$\underline{\hspace{3em}} + \underline{\hspace{3em}} = \underline{\hspace{3em}}$$

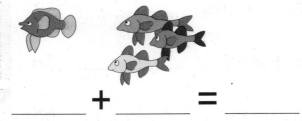

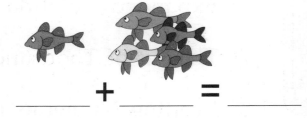

$$\underline{\hspace{3em}} + \underline{\hspace{3em}} = \underline{\hspace{3em}}$$

$$\underline{\hspace{3em}} + \underline{\hspace{3em}} = \underline{\hspace{3em}}$$

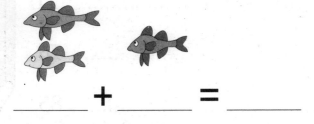

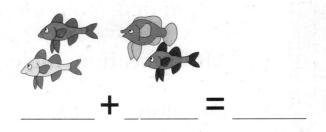

$$\underline{\hspace{3em}} + \underline{\hspace{3em}} = \underline{\hspace{3em}}$$

$$\underline{\hspace{3em}} + \underline{\hspace{3em}} = \underline{\hspace{3em}}$$

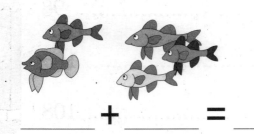

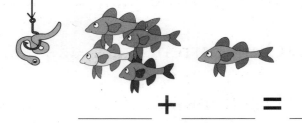

$$\underline{\hspace{3em}} + \underline{\hspace{3em}} = \underline{\hspace{3em}}$$

$$\underline{\hspace{3em}} + \underline{\hspace{3em}} = \underline{\hspace{3em}}$$

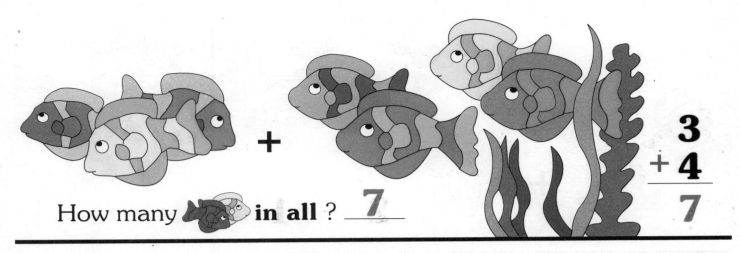

How many  **in all** ? ___7___

$$\begin{array}{r} 3 \\ +\,4 \\ \hline 7 \end{array}$$

Find the **sum.**

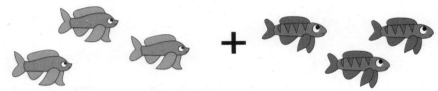

How many **in all** ? _____

$$\begin{array}{r} 5 \\ +\,2 \\ \hline \end{array}$$

How many **in all** ? _____

$$\begin{array}{r} 3 \\ +\,3 \\ \hline \end{array}$$

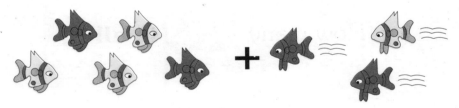

How many **in all** ? _____

$$\begin{array}{r} 5 \\ +\,3 \\ \hline \end{array}$$

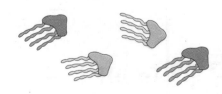

How many **in all** ? _____

$$\begin{array}{r} 4 \\ +\,4 \\ \hline \end{array}$$

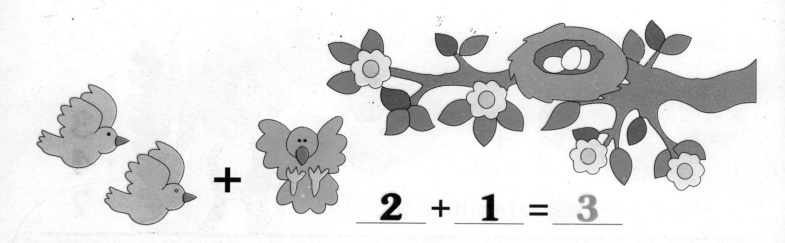

2 + 1 = 3

Count, **write** and then **add**.

_____ + _____ = _____

How many **in all** ? _____

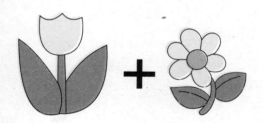

_____ + _____ = _____

How many **in all** ? _____

_____ + _____ = _____

How many **in all** ? _____

2 + **2** = **4**

in all

Count, write and then add.

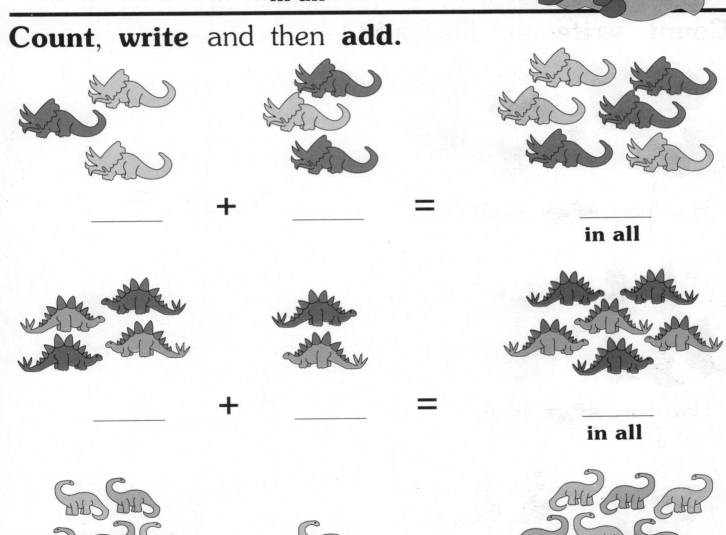

_____ + _____ = _____

in all

_____ + _____ = _____

in all

_____ + _____ = _____

in all

How many  in all ?   **2** + **4** = 6

Count, **write** and then **add.**

How many in all ?   _____ + _____ = _____

How many in all ?   _____ + _____ = _____

How many in all ?   _____ + _____ = _____

Let's add Bigger Numbers

Add the **units** first and then add the **tens**.

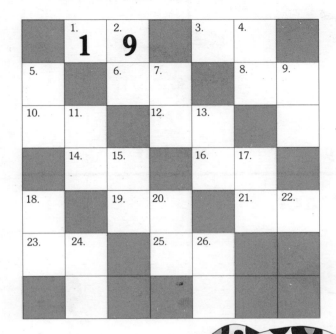

Across

1. $\begin{array}{r} 18 \\ +\ 1 \\ \hline 19 \end{array}$

3. $\begin{array}{r} 44 \\ +\ 2 \\ \hline \end{array}$

6. $\begin{array}{r} 38 \\ +\ 0 \\ \hline \end{array}$

8. $\begin{array}{r} 53 \\ +\ 4 \\ \hline \end{array}$

10. $\begin{array}{r} 31 \\ +\ 8 \\ \hline \end{array}$

12. $\begin{array}{r} 77 \\ +\ 2 \\ \hline \end{array}$

14. $\begin{array}{r} 45 \\ +\ 4 \\ \hline \end{array}$

16. $\begin{array}{r} 25 \\ +\ 3 \\ \hline \end{array}$

19. $\begin{array}{r} 20 \\ +\ 9 \\ \hline \end{array}$

21. $\begin{array}{r} 33 \\ +\ 3 \\ \hline \end{array}$

23. $\begin{array}{r} 85 \\ +\ 3 \\ \hline \end{array}$

25. $\begin{array}{r} 47 \\ +\ 2 \\ \hline \end{array}$

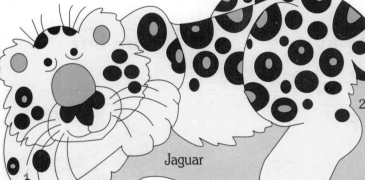

Jaguar

Down

2. $\begin{array}{r} 93 \\ +\ 0 \\ \hline \end{array}$

4. $\begin{array}{r} 63 \\ +\ 2 \\ \hline \end{array}$

5. $\begin{array}{r} 41 \\ +\ 2 \\ \hline \end{array}$

7. $\begin{array}{r} 84 \\ +\ 3 \\ \hline \end{array}$

9. $\begin{array}{r} 75 \\ +\ 4 \\ \hline \end{array}$

11. $\begin{array}{r} 92 \\ +\ 2 \\ \hline \end{array}$

13. $\begin{array}{r} 90 \\ +\ 2 \\ \hline \end{array}$

15. $\begin{array}{r} 91 \\ +\ 1 \\ \hline \end{array}$

17. $\begin{array}{r} 82 \\ +\ 1 \\ \hline \end{array}$

18. $\begin{array}{r} 55 \\ +\ 3 \\ \hline \end{array}$

20. $\begin{array}{r} 74 \\ +\ 20 \\ \hline \end{array}$

24. $\begin{array}{r} 86 \\ +\ 3 \\ \hline \end{array}$

26. $\begin{array}{r} 95 \\ +\ 3 \\ \hline \end{array}$

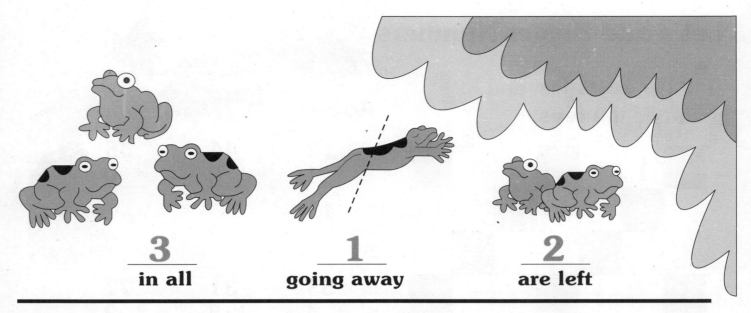

3 in all **1** going away **2** are left

Count, write and then subtract.

_____ in all _____ going away _____ are left

_____ in all _____ going away _____ are left

_____ in all _____ going away _____ are left

7
in all

7 – **3** = **4**
in all   are left

Count, write and then subtract.

_____
in all

_____ – _____ = _____
in all   are left

_____
in all

_____ – _____ = _____
in all   are left

_____
in all

_____ – _____ = _____
in all   are left

Count, subtract and then write
the **remainder**.

How many frogs **are left** ?

3 frogs

How many cats **are left** ?

_____ cats

How many rabbits **are left** ?

_____ rabbits

How many dogs **are left** ?

_____ dogs

How many mice **are left** ?

_____ mice

How many sparrows **are left** ?

_____ birds

Count, **subtract** and then write the **remainder**.

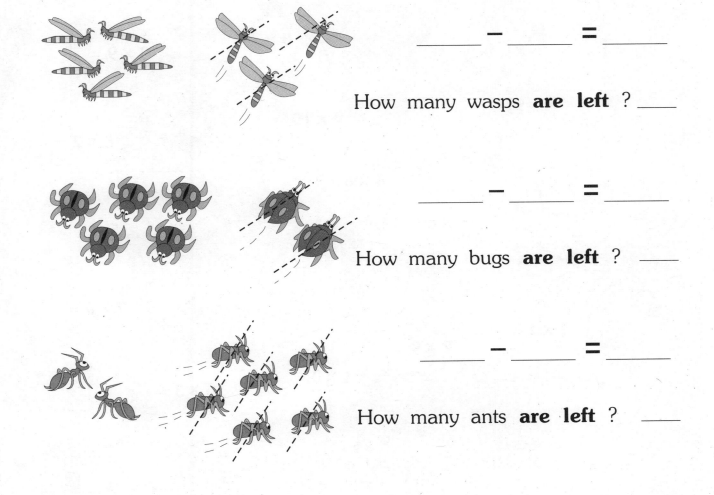

_____ – _____ = _____

How many wasps **are left** ? ____

_____ – _____ = _____

How many bugs **are left** ? ____

_____ – _____ = _____

How many ants **are left** ? ____

_____ – _____ = _____

How many bees **are left** ? ____

Multiplication Tables : Revision

6 × 7 =

7 × 3 =

3 × 4 =

0 × 7 =

9 × 9 =

8 × 8 =

9 × 10 =

8 × 2 =

2 × 7 =

4 × 6 =

5 × 8 =

5 × 5 =

4 × 4 =

7 × 6 =

2 × 9 =

6 × 5 =

1 × 0 =

10 × 3 =

9 × 4 =

6 × 10 =

10 × 10 =

8 × 7 =

3 × 3 =

Multiply the following numbers.

3 × 2 =

3 × 9 =

4 × 5 =

4 × 9 =

5 × 6 =

5 × 9 =

6 × 2 =

6 × 7 =

7 × 4 =

7 × 8 =

Ruby-topaz Hummingbird

Praying Mantis

```
    9          9
  × 4        × 9
_____     _____
```

```
   10         10
 ×  5       ×  8
_____     _____
```

```
    5          5
  × 3        × 4
_____     _____
```

```
    8          6
  × 4        × 6
_____     _____
```

Fill up the **missing number.**

$5 \times \rule{1cm}{0.4pt} = 20$

$9 \times \rule{1cm}{0.4pt} = 63$

$9 \times \rule{1cm}{0.4pt} = 9$

$10 \times \rule{1cm}{0.4pt} = 40$

$\rule{1cm}{0.4pt} \times 8 = 32$

$\rule{1cm}{0.4pt} \times 4 = 24$

$9 \times \rule{1cm}{0.4pt} = 81$

$6 \times \rule{1cm}{0.4pt} = 42$

$\rule{1cm}{0.4pt} \times 7 = 14$

$\rule{1cm}{0.4pt} \times 7 = 49$

$\rule{1cm}{0.4pt} \times 10 = 90$

$\rule{1cm}{0.4pt} \times 10 = 50$

$3 \times \rule{1cm}{0.4pt} = 24$

$9 \times \rule{1cm}{0.4pt} = 72$

$4 \times \rule{1cm}{0.4pt} = 12$

$8 \times \rule{1cm}{0.4pt} = 64$

Brown Bear

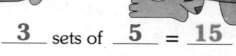

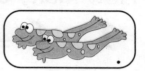
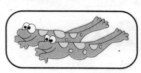

___3___ sets of ___5___ = ___15___

___5___ + ___5___ + ___5___ = ___15___

Three sets of Five

___3___ × ___5___ = ___15___

Now fill up the **blanks.**

_____ sets of _____ = _____

_____ + _____ = _____

Two sets of Two

_____ × _____ = _____

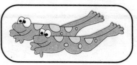
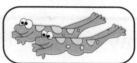

_____ sets of _____ = _____

_____ + _____ + _____ + _____ = _____

Four sets of Two

_____ × _____ = _____

_____ sets of _____ = _____

_____ + _____ + _____ = _____

Three sets of Three

_____ × _____ = _____

_____ sets of _____ = _____

_____ + _____ + _____ + _____ = _____

Four sets of Four

_____ × _____ = _____

Multiplication and Addition

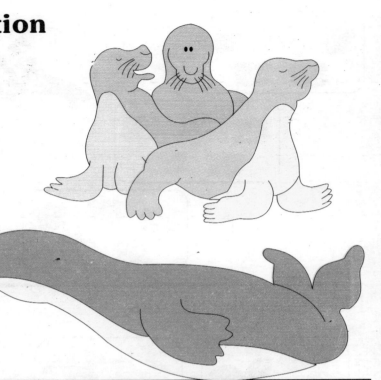

4 + 4 + 4 = 12

How many **4**'s ? ___**3**___

___**3**___ x ___**4**___ = ___**12**___

6 + 6 + 6 + 6 = 24

How many **6**'s ? ___**4**___

___**4**___ x ___**6**___ = ___**24**___

Now fill up the **blanks**.

2 + 2 + 2 + 2 = 8

___ × ___ = ___

5 + 5 + 5 + 5 + 5 + 5 = 30

___ × ___ = ___

1 + 1 + 1 + 1 = 4

___ × ___ = ___

6 + 6 + 6 = 18

___ × ___ = ___

3 + 3 + 3 + 3 = 12

___ × ___ = ___

4 + 4 = 8

___ × ___ = ___

9 + 9 = 18

___ × ___ = ___

7 + 7 + 7 = 21

___ × ___ = ___

2 sets.
3 in each set.
2 × 3 = 6

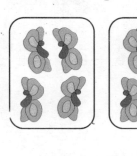

Now fill up the **blanks.**

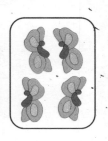   

_____ × _____ = _____   _____ × _____ = _____

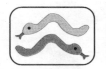

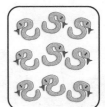      

_____ × _____ = _____   _____ × _____ = _____

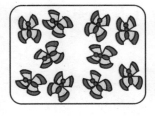   

_____ × _____ = _____   _____ × _____ = _____

Add or Multiply

We **repeat addition** when we **multiply**.

$3 \times 2 = 6$

$2 + 2 + 2 = 6$

Ocelot

Now fill up the **blanks.**

$4 \times 4 = 16$

___ + ___ + ___ + ___ = ___

$3 + 3 + 3 + 3 + 3 = 15$

___ × ___ = ___

$5 \times 9 = 45$

___ + ___ + ___ + ___ + ___ = ___

$6 + 6 + 6 + 6 + 6 + 6 = 36$

___ × ___ = ___

$3 \times 3 = 9$

___ + ___ + ___ = ___

$8 + 8 = 16$

___ × ___ = ___

$3 \times 7 = 21$

___ + ___ + ___ = ___

$7 + 7 + 7 + 7 = 28$

___ × ___ = ___

$5 \times 7 = 35$

___ + ___ + ___ + ___ + ___ = ___

$9 + 9 + 9 + 9 + 9 = 45$

___ × ___ = ___

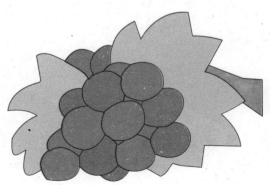

Write the **product**.

2 × 1 = _____   3 × 1 = _____

2 × 2 = _____   3 × 2 = _____

2 × 3 = _____   3 × 3 = _____

2 × 4 = _____   3 × 4 = _____

2 × 5 = _____   3 × 5 = _____

2 × 6 = _____   3 × 6 = _____

2 × 7 = _____   3 × 7 = _____

2 × 8 = _____   3 × 8 = _____

2 × 9 = _____   3 × 9 = _____

2 × 10 = _____   3 × 10 = _____

Note : We get the same answer in multiplication, even if the order
of the numbers is changed.

2 sets of **5** and **5** sets of **2** have the same
answers, i.e. **2 × 5 = 10** or **5 × 2 = 10.**

2 × 4 = _____   4 × 2 = _____

3 × 6 = _____   6 × 3 = _____

3 × 4 = _____   4 × 3 = _____

7 × 2 = _____   2 × 7 = _____

2 × 3 = _____   3 × 2 = _____

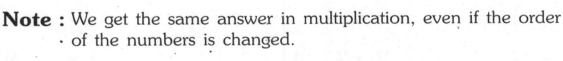

Toucan

Long- tongued Fruit Bat

Write the **product.**

4 × 1 = _____	5 × 1 = _____
4 × 2 = _____	5 × 2 = _____
4 × 3 = _____	5 × 3 = _____
4 × 4 = _____	5 × 4 = _____
4 × 5 = _____	5 × 5 = _____
4 × 6 = _____	5 × 6 = _____
4 × 7 = _____	5 × 7 = _____
4 × 8 = _____	5 × 8 = _____
4 × 9 = _____	5 × 9 = _____
4 × 10 = _____	5 × 10 = _____

Draw sets.

2 × 3 = 6
(2 sets of 3)

2 × 2 = 4
(2 sets of 2)

2 × 4 = 8
(2 sets of 4)

3 × 2 = 6
(3 sets of 2)

5 × 1 = 5
(5 sets of 1)

1 × 3 = 3
(1 set of 3)

Write the **product**.

6 × 1 = _____   7 × 1 = _____

6 × 2 = _____   7 × 2 = _____

6 × 3 = _____   7 × 3 = _____

6 × 4 = _____   7 × 4 = _____

6 × 5 = _____   7 × 5 = _____

6 × 6 = _____   7 × 6 = _____

6 × 7 = _____   7 × 7 = _____

6 × 8 = _____   7 × 8 = _____

6 × 9 = _____   7 × 9 = _____

6 × 10 = _____   7 × 10 = _____

Red Howler
Monkey

Multiply as shown in the example below.

6 sets of **4** = <u> **6 X 4 = 24** </u>

2 sets of **7** = _____

6 sets of **7** = _____

5 sets of **6** = _____

8 sets of **7** = _____

7 sets of **3** = _____

6 sets of **8** = _____

4 sets of **7** = _____

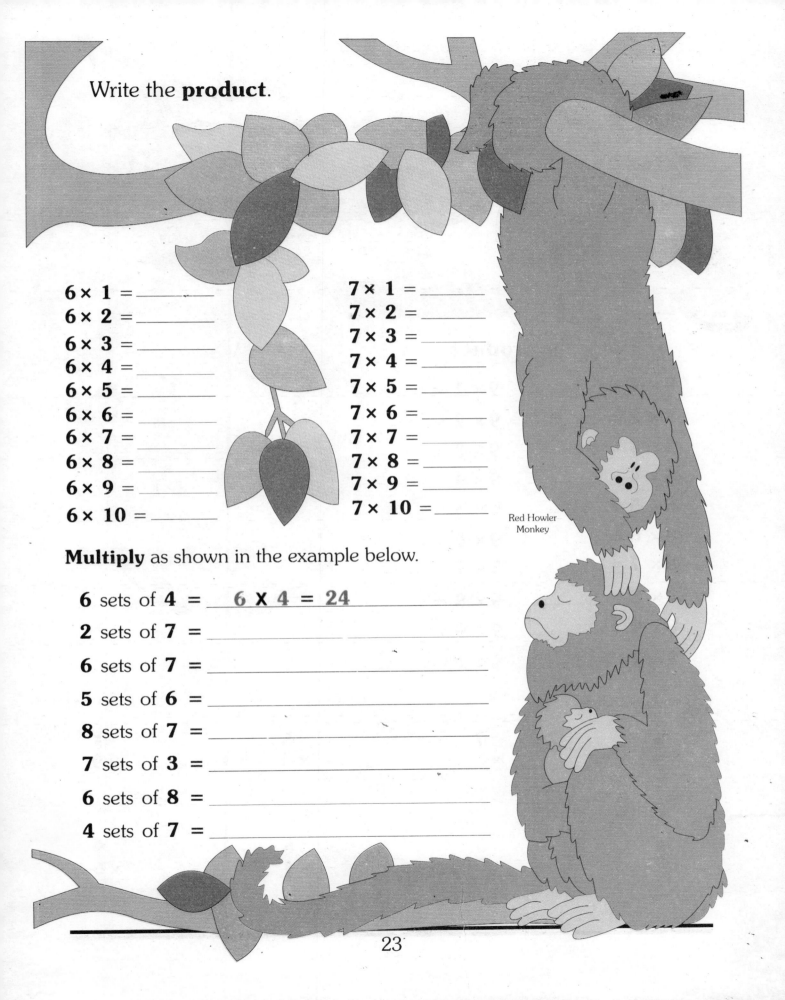

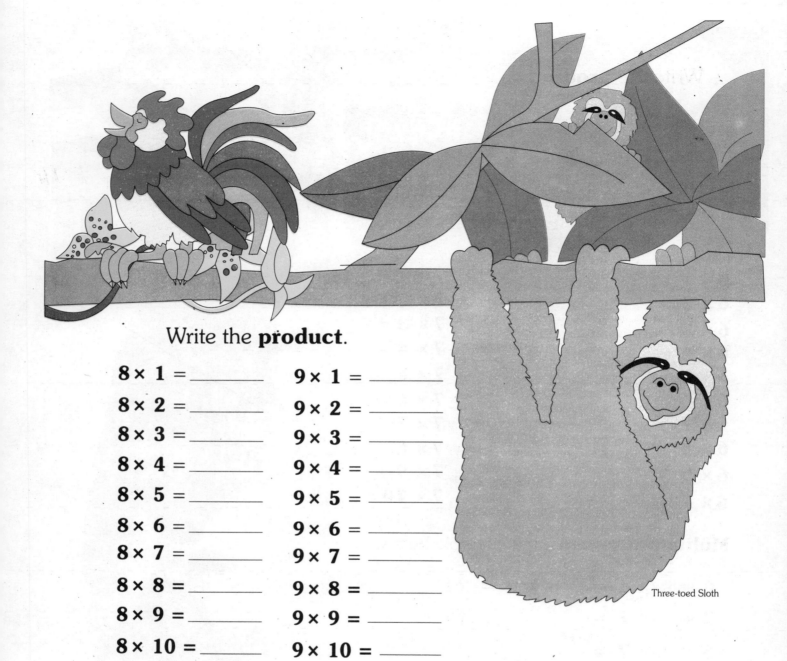

Write the **product**.

8 × 1 = _____	9 × 1 = _____
8 × 2 = _____	9 × 2 = _____
8 × 3 = _____	9 × 3 = _____
8 × 4 = _____	9 × 4 = _____
8 × 5 = _____	9 × 5 = _____
8 × 6 = _____	9 × 6 = _____
8 × 7 = _____	9 × 7 = _____
8 × 8 = _____	9 × 8 = _____
8 × 9 = _____	9 × 9 = _____
8 × 10 = _____	9 × 10 = _____

Three-toed Sloth

Review

4	7	8	5
× 4	× 3	× 4	× 9

4	3	6	9
× 7	× 5	× 4	× 6

Koala

Rainbow Lory

Let's revise our **multiplication tables** first and then find the **product.**

$8 \times 9 =$ _____ $10 \times 10 =$ _____ $9 \times 7 =$ _____

$6 \times 7 =$ _____ $8 \times 6 =$ _____ $10 \times 7 =$ _____

$9 \times 5 =$ _____ $10 \times 4 =$ _____ $6 \times 4 =$ _____

$8 \times 8 =$ _____ $7 \times 5 =$ _____ $10 \times 6 =$ _____

$9 \times 9 =$ _____ $8 \times 4 =$ _____ $7 \times 7 =$ _____

$6 \times 3 =$ _____ $10 \times 3 =$ _____ $6 \times 9 =$ _____

$8 \times 7 =$ _____ $10 \times 2 =$ _____ $8 \times 2 =$ _____

$7 \times 3 =$ _____ $7 \times 4 =$ _____ $10 \times 9 =$ _____

$6 \times 6 =$ _____ $9 \times 9 =$ _____ $10 \times 5 =$ _____

Read each set of **numerals**.
Write them in **order** from the
least to the **greatest**.

Northern Pocket
Gopher

12	10	15		45	49	36
___	___	___		___	___	___
81	19	25		36	24	18
___	___	___		___	___	___
29	57	41		30	72	55
___	___	___		___	___	___
66	26	56		87	78	72
___	___	___		___	___	___

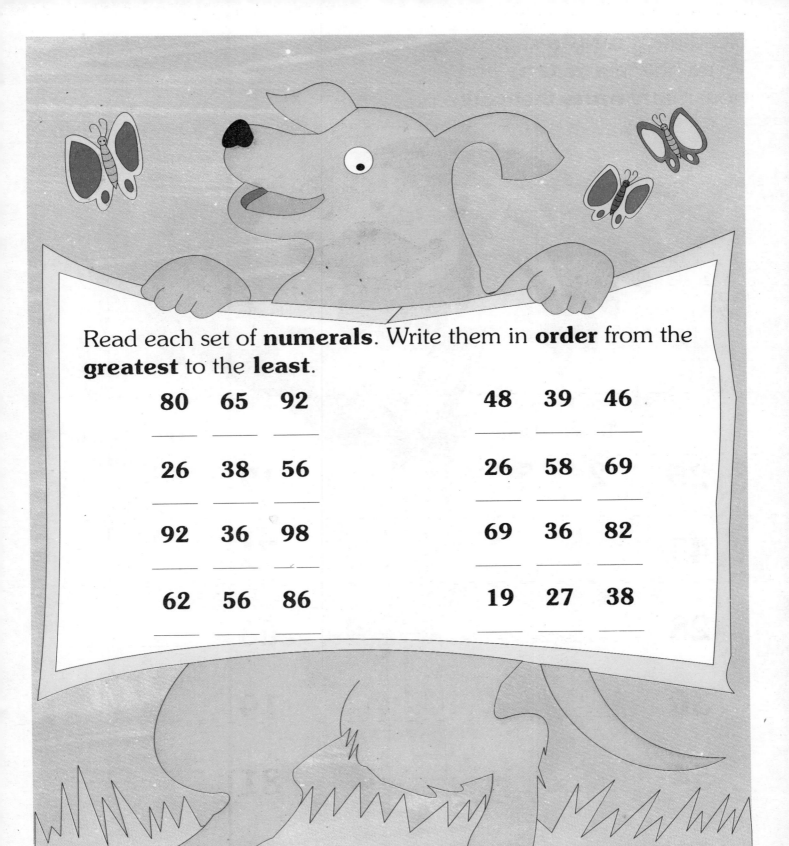

Read each set of **numerals**. Write them in **order** from the **greatest** to the **least**.

80	65	92		48	39	46
_____	_____	_____		_____	_____	_____
26	38	56		26	58	69
_____	_____	_____		_____	_____	_____
92	36	98		69	36	82
_____	_____	_____		_____	_____	_____
62	56	86		19	27	38
_____	_____	_____		_____	_____	_____

Read each **number**.
Write how many **tens** and
how many **units** there are.

	Tens	Units
25	2	5
43		
28		
30		
54		
65		

	Tens	Units
17		
71		
66		
19		
81		
40		

Write the correct **numeral**.

2 tens and **6** units ___26___   **4** tens and **5** units = _____

4 tens and **1** unit _____   **5** tens and **3** units = _____

7 tens and **0** unit _____   **1** ten and **9** units _____

2 tens and **5** units _____   **6** tens and **4** units _____

0 ten and **8** units _____   **9** tens and **2** units _____

8 tens and **6** units _____   **5** tens and **0** unit _____

3 tens and **7** units _____   **2** tens and **2** units _____

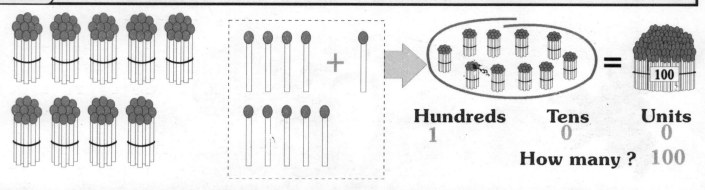

	Hundreds	Tens	Units
	1	0	0
How many ?			100

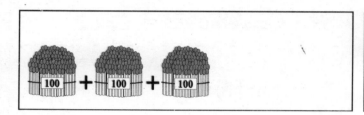

Hundreds	Tens	Units	
2	0	0	200

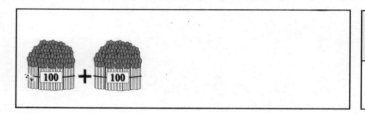

Hundreds	Tens	Units	
3	0	0	300

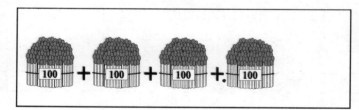

Hundreds	Tens	Units	
4	0	0	400

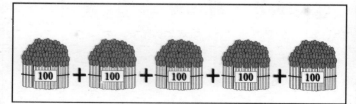

Hundreds	Tens	Units	
5	0	0	500

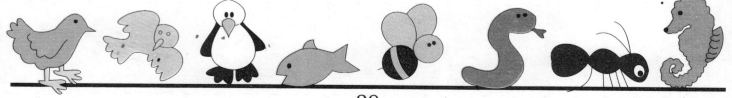

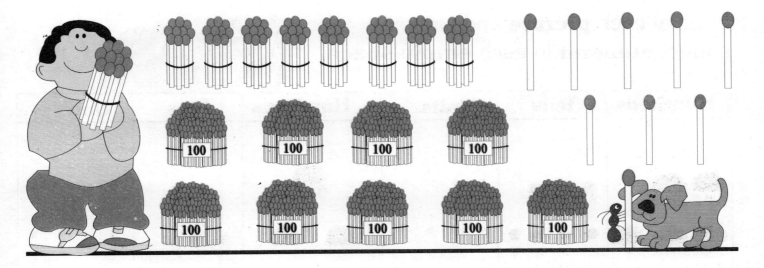

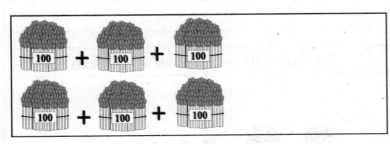

Hundreds	Tens	Units
6	0	0

600

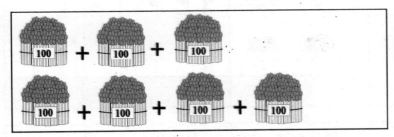

Hundreds	Tens	Units
7	0	0

700

Hundreds	Tens	Units
8	0	0

800

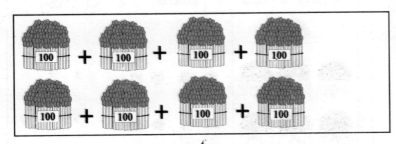

Hundreds	Tens	Units
9	0	0

900

Look at each **picture** and write the correct **numeral** in each **empty space**.

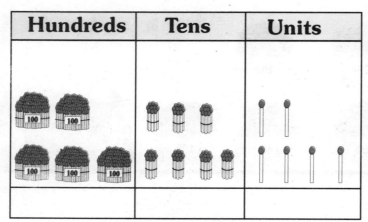

Black Panther

Hundreds	Tens	Units

Hundreds	Tens	Units

Hundreds	Tens	Units

Hundreds	Tens	Units

Hundreds	Tens	Units

Hundreds	Tens	Units

Egret

Let's know more about **Hundreds, Tens** and **units**.

296 = 2 9 6
(Hundreds Tens Units)

Now read each **numeral** and then **circle** the **correct answer**.

Cheetah

Which number shows **4** hundreds ? 324 (422) 243

Which number shows **2** hundreds ? 280 120 342

Which number shows **8** hundreds ? 618 580 800

Which number shows **5** hundreds ? 125 251 512

Which number shows **1** hundred ? 180 801 810

Which number shows **9** hundreds ? 490 966 489

Which number shows **3** hundreds ? 324 833 133

Which number shows **6** hundreds ? 465 678 396

Which number shows **7** hundreds ? 700 570 897

Which number shows **5** hundreds ? 205 355 555

Which number shows **0** hundred ? 180 510 90

Which number shows **9** hundreds ? 192 944 899

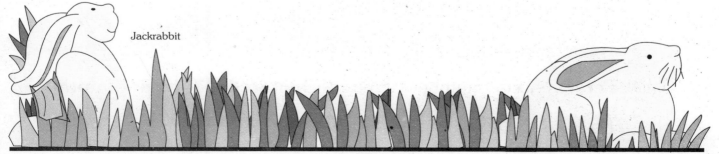

Jackrabbit

Read each **statement** and then **circle** the correct **digit.**

Circle the **hundreds.** 4 8 7

Circle the **units.** 2 8 9

Circle the **hundreds.** 3 3 3

Circle the **tens.** 8 2 5

Circle the **tens.** 4 0 0

Circle the **hundreds.** 8 9 9

Circle the **hundreds.** 2 1 5

Circle the **tens.** 4 5 8

Circle the **units.** 5 7 0

Circle the **units.** 8 6 7

Circle the **hundreds.** 6 4 8

Circle the **tens.** 4 4 4

Circle **Peter's** house number. It has **9 hundreds 7 tens 6 units.**

785   976   765   997   796

Adding Hundreds, Tens and Units with carrying over digits.

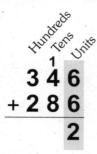

```
  Hundreds          Hundreds          Hundreds
    Tens              Tens              Tens
     Units             Units             Units
    1                1 1              1 1
  3 4 6            3 4 6            3 4 6
+ 2 8 6          + 2 8 6          + 2 8 6
_____          _____          _____
      2              3 2          6 3 2
```

1. Add the **units**.
6 + 6 = 12
12 is **1 ten**
and **2 units**.

2. Add the **tens**.
Don't forget
the **1 ten**.
1 + 4 + 8 = 13

3. Add the **hundreds**.
Don't forget the
1 hundred.
1 + 3 + 2 = 6

Therefore the **sum** is : **632** or 6 hundreds
3 tens 2 units.

Find the **sum**.

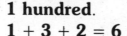

221 + 579	398 + 352	375 + 246	200 + 200
519 + 399	600 + 300	634 + 200	721 + 189
496 + 366	100 + 500	519 + 181	131 + 689
700 + 197	400 + 450	647 + 188	200 + 600

Green Turtle

Leatherback
Turtle

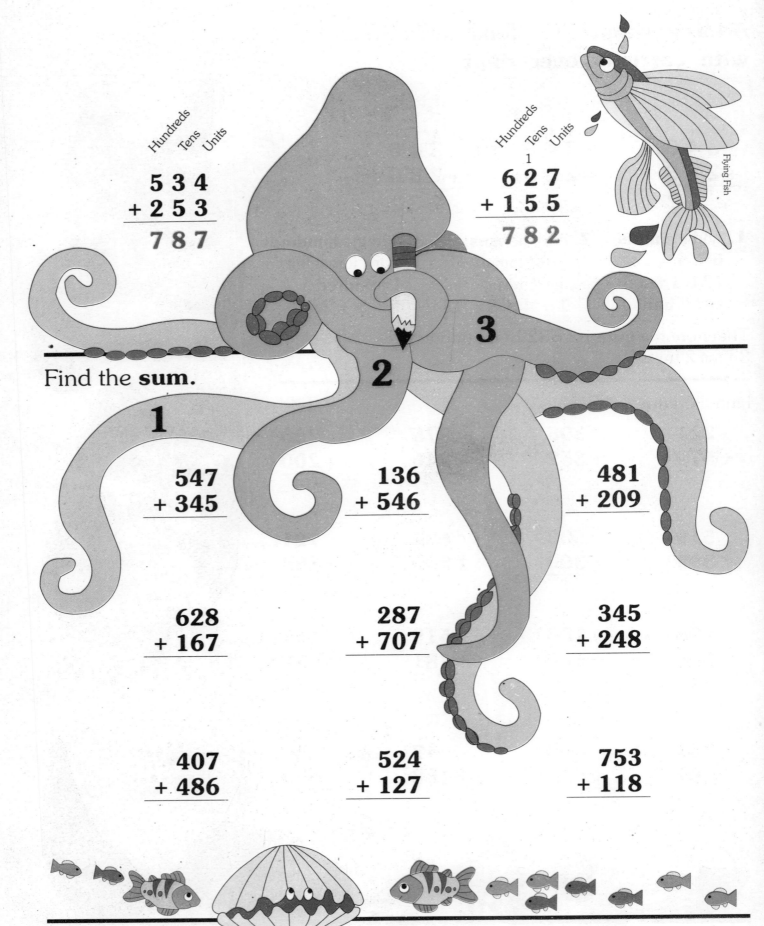

Hundreds	Tens	Units
5	3	4
+ 2	5	3
7	8	7

Flying Fish

Hundreds	Tens	Units
	1	
6	2	7
+ 1	5	5
7	8	2

Find the **sum.**

1

$$547 + 345$$

2

$$136 + 546$$

3

$$481 + 209$$

$$628 + 167$$

$$287 + 707$$

$$345 + 248$$

$$407 + 486$$

$$524 + 127$$

$$753 + 118$$

Find the **sum.**

845 + 150	420 + 594	864 + 100	915 + 270
872 + 443	584 + 372	240 + 495	798 + 114
236 + 485	591 + 147	278 + 243	632 + 287
696 + 200	745 + 187	188 + 181	276 + 575

Find the **sum**.

188 + 10	244 + 23	852 + 34	205 + 41
428 + 23	107 + 10	314 + 48	239 + 25
132 +400	37 +135	650 +125	175 +200
125 +470	447 + 38	436 + 45	546 +137

Blue Wildebeest

Egret

Subtracting Hundreds, Tens and Units with borrowing digits.

```
       Hundreds  Tens  Units
                  2     18
          6       3     8
      -   2       0     9
                        9
```

As we can't subtract 9 units from 8 units, we shall borrow 1 ten out of 3 tens. So, we shall have 10 + 8 = 18 units in all.

```
       Hundreds  Tens  Units
                  2     18
          6       3     8
      -   2       0     9
                  2     9
```

Now we can subtract 9 units from 18 units to get 9 units as their difference. Now we have 2 tens left. On subtracting 0 ten from 2 tens we get 2 tens.

```
       Hundreds  Tens  Units
                  2     18
          6       3     8
      -   2       0     9
          4       2     9
```

Now subtract the hundreds.

Find the **remainder**.

148 − 36	174 − 43	243 − 33	255 − 48
353 −205	326 −250	870 −328	258 −146
694 −589	786 −579	971 − 26	777 −456
219 − 14	493 −188	800 −250	550 −315

Hippopotamus

Find the **remainder**.

146	813	486	333
− 22	− 12	− 74	− 12

750	681	175	926
−400	−351	−114	−422

487	593	296	758
− 29	−162	− 89	−135

832	485	398	459
−109	−368	−250	− 47

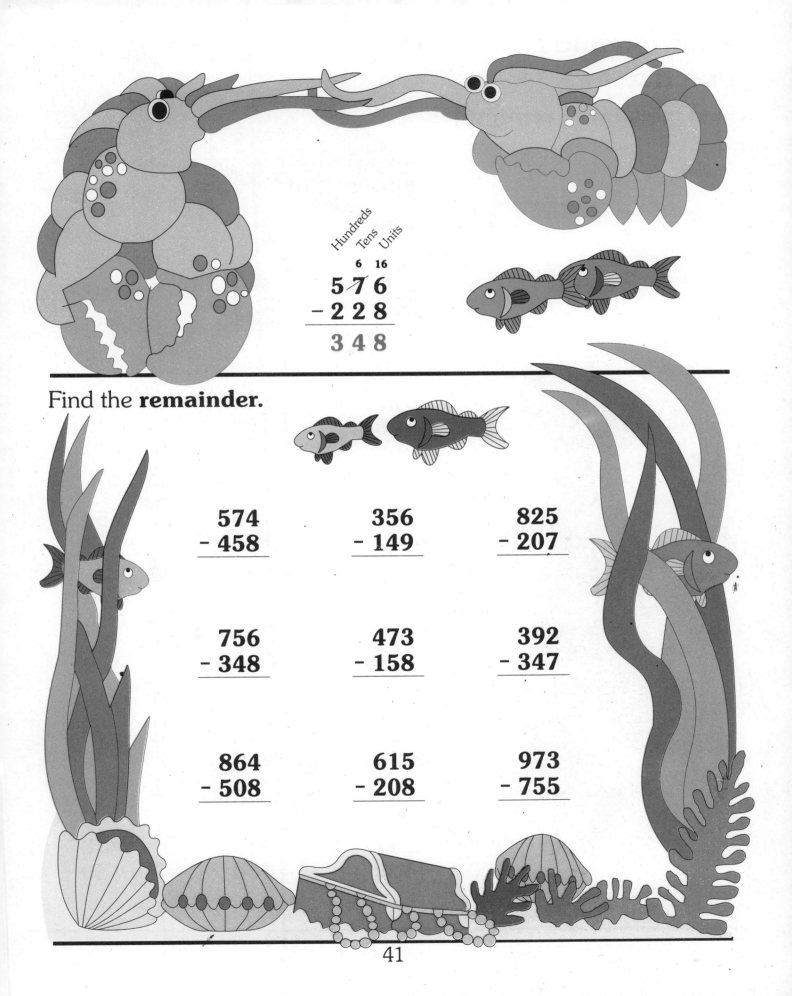

Hundreds   Tens   Units

$$
\begin{array}{r}
\overset{6\ \ 16}{5\,7\,6} \\
-\,2\,2\,8 \\
\hline
3\,4\,8
\end{array}
$$

Find the **remainder.**

574	356	825
− 458	− 149	− 207

756	473	392
− 348	− 158	− 347

864	615	973
− 508	− 208	− 755

Addition and Subtraction Practice - I

Find the **sum** or **remainder**.

Sei Whale

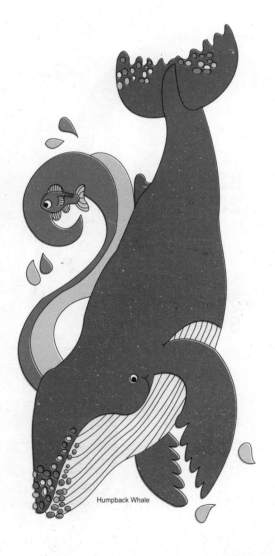
Humpback Whale

585 − 269	274 + 234	108 + 544
922 − 108	184 + 507	355 − 118
571 + 262	963 − 125	456 + 138
222 − 115	753 + 156	151 − 138
260 + 480	990 − 480	926 − 425
251 + 492	926 − 380	442 + 480

Addition and Subtraction Practice - II

Put a **cross** (✗) on each **incorrect answer**.

64	36	387
+23	+27	+116
97	63	496

84	73	460
−36	−27	−129
98	46	342

39	47	392
+25	+35	+138
64	82	496

79	83	467
−34	−36	−139
35	47	329

39	44	384
+27	+38	+127
66	86	511

88	60	452
−39	−27	−137
49	33	325

Addition and Subtraction
Practice - III

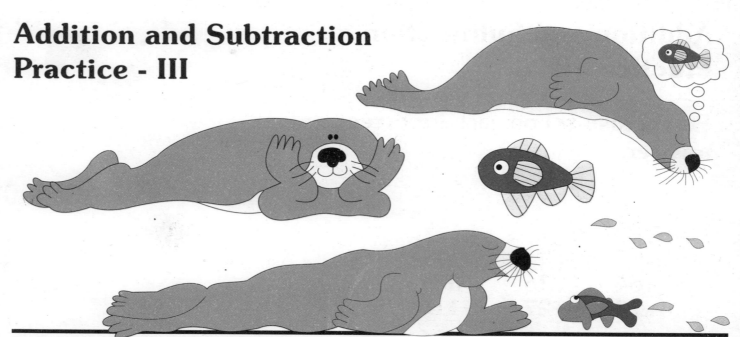

Find the **sum** or **remainder** and **circle** the correct answer.

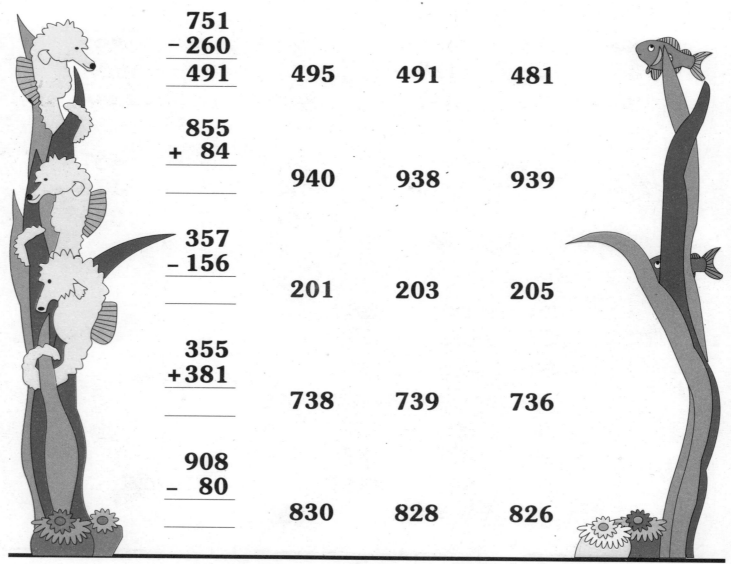

751 − 260 491	495	491	481
855 + 84	940	938	939
357 − 156	201	203	205
355 + 381	738	739	736
908 − 80	830	828	826

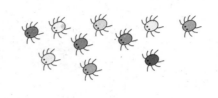

$$239 = \begin{matrix} \text{Hundreds} & \text{Tens} & \text{Units} \\ 2 & 3 & 9 \end{matrix}$$

So, the numeral 239 contains two hundreds(200)+three tens(30)+nine units(9) or 200+30+9 = 239.

Now **read** and **write** the following **numerals** :

	Hundreds	Tens	Units
400	_____	_____	_____
169	_____	_____	_____
208	_____	_____	_____
284	_____	_____	_____
883	_____	_____	_____
912	_____	_____	_____
734	_____	_____	_____
250	_____	_____	_____
188	_____	_____	_____
999	_____	_____	_____

Words to Numerals

Two hundreds seven tens eight units

$$278 = 2 \quad 7 \quad 8$$

Hundreds Tens Units

Make numerals from the following :

Three hundreds two tens one unit = __321__

Five hundreds six tens zero unit = _____

Nine hundreds five tens two units = _____

Seven hundreds zero ten two units = _____

Six hundreds one ten three units = _____

Eight hundreds six tens zero unit = _____

One hundred one ten one unit = _____

Nine hundreds nine tens nine units = _____

Eight hundreds nine tens nine units = _____

Six hundreds zero ten zero unit = _____

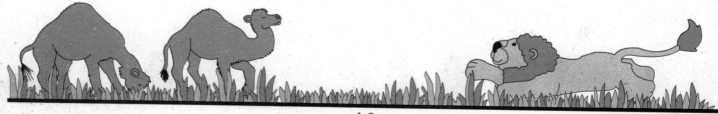

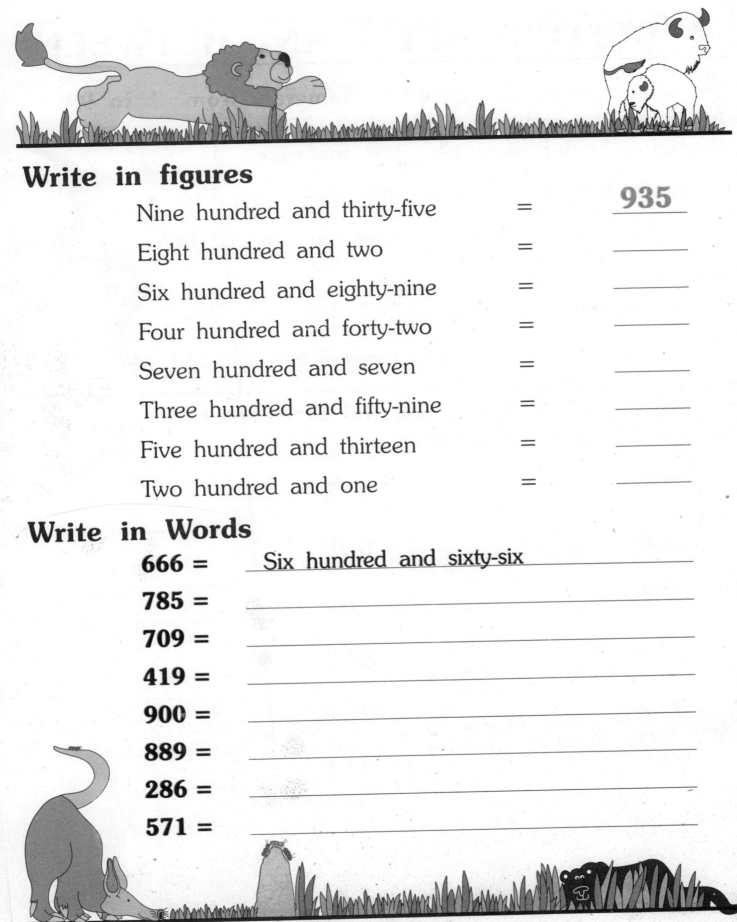

Write in figures

Nine hundred and thirty-five = <u>935</u>

Eight hundred and two = _____

Six hundred and eighty-nine = _____

Four hundred and forty-two = _____

Seven hundred and seven = _____

Three hundred and fifty-nine = _____

Five hundred and thirteen = _____

Two hundred and one = _____

Write in Words

666 = <u>Six hundred and sixty-six</u>

785 = _____

709 = _____

419 = _____

900 = _____

889 = _____

286 = _____

571 = _____

4 BEFORE, AFTER AND BETWEEN

We have known the order of numerals from 1 to 99. After every hundred (100, 200, 300,........... etc), the same order goes on. For instance,

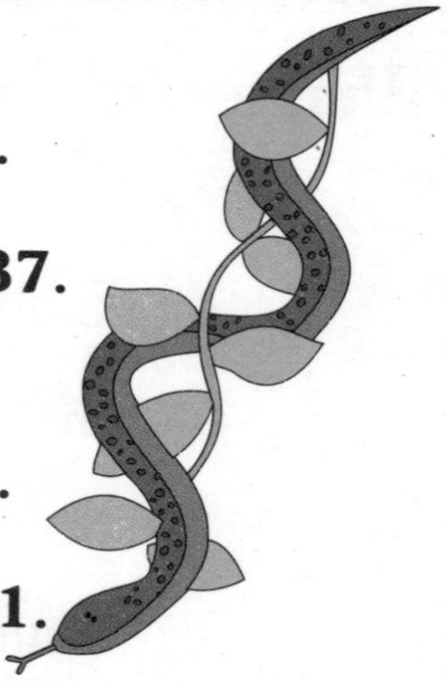

Before **136** comes **135** and after **136** comes **137**.
Or
We can say that **136** comes between **135** and **137**.

Similarly ——

Before **300** comes **299** and after **300** comes **301**.
Or
We can say that **300** comes between **299** and **301**.

Fill up the box with the numeral that comes before the given numeral.

309		**473**	
500		**999**	
138		**387**	
645		**867**	
912		**260**	
765		**344**	

Fill up the box with the numeral that comes after the given numeral.

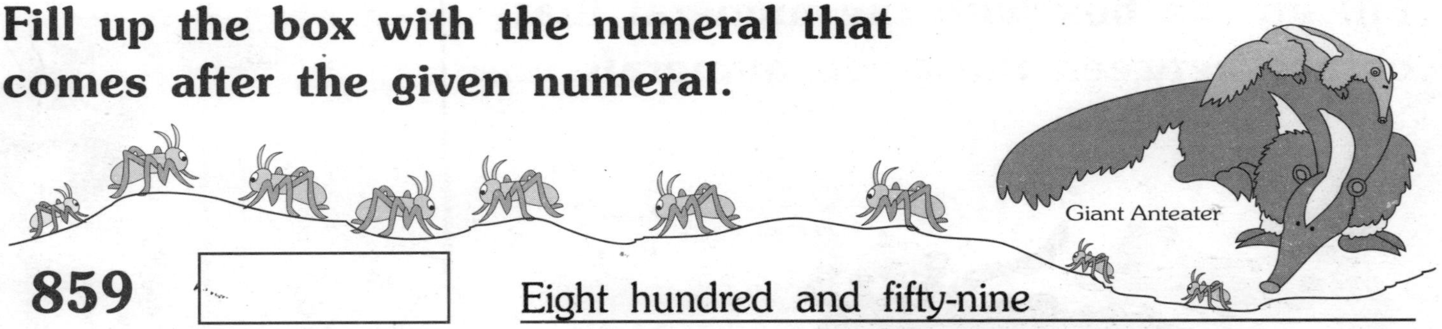

859 ☐ <u>Eight hundred and fifty-nine</u>

Giant Anteater

248 ☐ _____

743 ☐ _____

664 ☐ _____

369 ☐ _____

899 ☐ _____

326 ☐ _____

905 ☐ _____

333 ☐ _____

872 ☐ _____

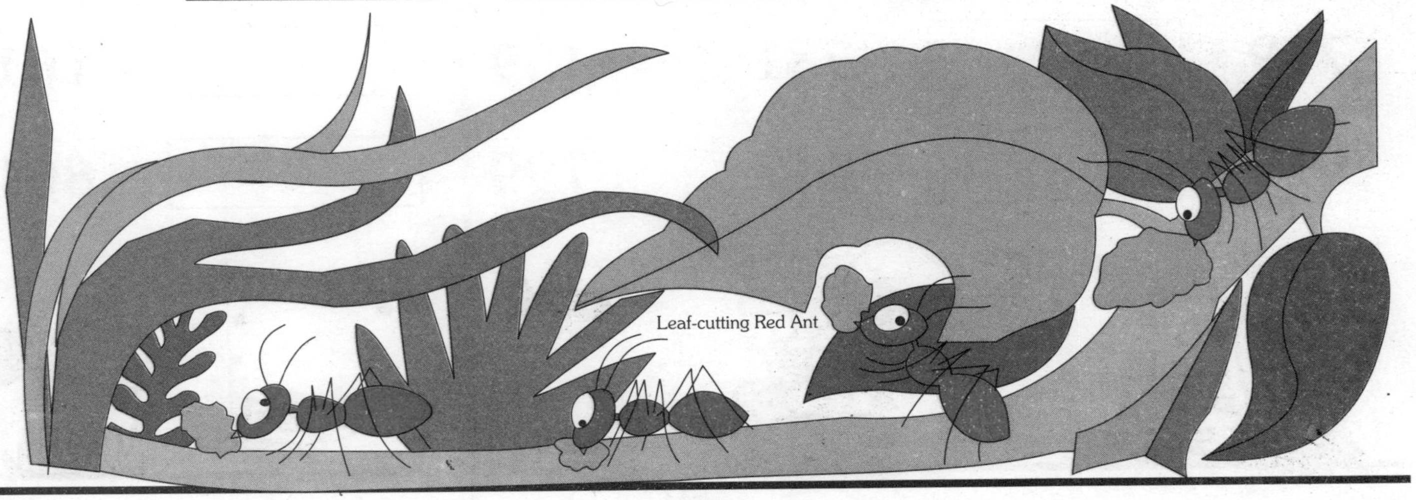

Leaf-cutting Red Ant

Fill up the box with the numeral that comes between the given numerals.

569		571	398		400
883		885	309		311
944		946	620		622
589		591	200		202
299		301	569		571
568		570	219		221
290		292	106		108
438		440	789		791
779		781	159		161
615		617	799		801

5 COMPARING NUMBERS

< means **less** than. **<**

> means **greater** than. **>**

= means **equal**.  **=**

Now use one of the signs to **compare** the numbers below.

687 _____ 593   254 _____ 221   10 × 6 _____ 8 × 8

521 _____ 843   333 _____ 349   20 − 6 _____ 2 × 7

754 _____ 926   905 _____ 926   10 + 9 _____ 5 × 5

Put the numbers in order from the **least** to the **greatest**.

149	822	324	287	450
....	....	....	....	....

297	300	211	365	169
....	....	....	....	....

443	840	931	821	720
....	....	....	....	....

859	560	670	717	480
....	....	....	....	....

999	756	900	567	235
....	....	....	....	....

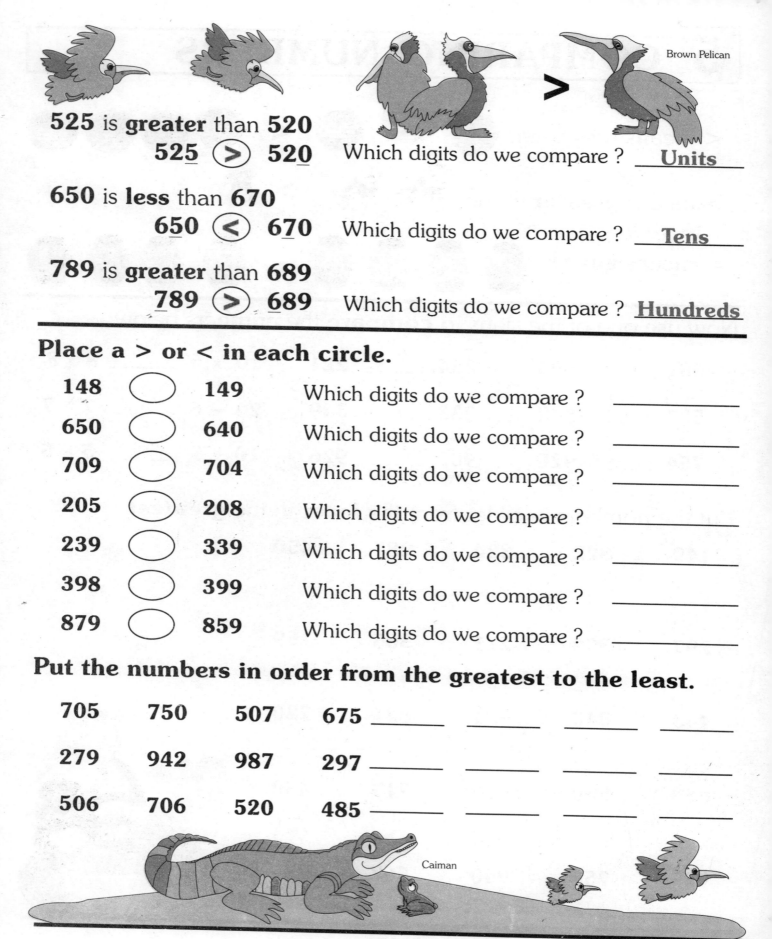

Brown Pelican

525 is **greater** than 520

525 ⊖ 520   Which digits do we compare? __Units__

650 is **less** than 670

650 ⊖ 670   Which digits do we compare? __Tens__

789 is **greater** than 689

789 ⊖ 689   Which digits do we compare? **Hundreds**

Place a > or < in each circle.

148 ◯ 149   Which digits do we compare? _____

650 ◯ 640   Which digits do we compare? _____

709 ◯ 704   Which digits do we compare? _____

205 ◯ 208   Which digits do we compare? _____

239 ◯ 339   Which digits do we compare? _____

398 ◯ 399   Which digits do we compare? _____

879 ◯ 859   Which digits do we compare? _____

Put the numbers in order from the greatest to the least.

705   750   507   675 _____ _____ _____ _____

279   942   987   297 _____ _____ _____ _____

506   706   520   485 _____ _____ _____ _____

Caiman

6 EXPANDED NOTATION & PLACE VALUE

Let's write **372** in **expanded notation** using **numerals**.

$$372 = 300 + 70 + 2$$

Let's write **372** in **expanded notation** using **words**.

$$372 = 3 \text{ Hundreds} + 7 \text{ Tens} + 2 \text{ Units}$$

Write the following numbers in **expanded notation** using **numerals**.

562 = _____ + _____ + _____

953 = _____ + _____ + _____

375 = _____ + _____ + _____

617 = _____ + _____ + _____

109 = _____ + _____ + _____

Polar Bear

Write the following numbers in **expanded notation** using **words**.

109 = _____ + _____ + _____

514 = _____ + _____ + _____

936 = _____ + _____ + _____

398 = _____ + _____ + _____

617 = _____ + _____ + _____

We can also write the **expanded notation** in the form of a **numeral**.

For instance, $60 + 4 = 64$

$800 + 50 + 2 = 852$

Write each **expanded notation** in the form of a **numeral**.

$900 + 70 + 3 =$ ___973___

$800 + 80 + 4 =$ _____

$600 + 20 + 7 =$ _____

$400 + 60 + 5 =$ _____

$700 + 50 + 9 =$ _____

$200 + 40 + 8 =$ _____

$500 + 30 + 1 =$ _____

$300 + 90 + 2 =$ _____

$100 + 50 + 6 =$ _____

Place Value

The **face value** of a digit is the digit itself, whereas the **place value** of a digit is the value that it has by virtue of its place in a numeral. For example —

In **35**, the digit **3** has **one digit** to its right. So, its **place value** is **30**. But its **face value** is **3** (*the number itself*).

Note : *The place value of 0 is always equal to its face value, i.e. 0. It never changes whatever its place in a numeral.*

Write the **place value** of each **digit** in each **number.**

793

7 = _____

9 = _____

3 = _____

436

4 = _____

3 = _____

6 = _____

Fill up the **empty box.**

	in **251**	in **512**
Place value of **1**		
Place value of **2**		
Place value of **5**		

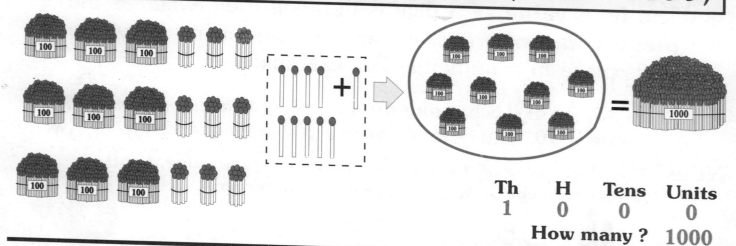

Th	H	Tens	Units
1	0	0	0

How many ? 1000

Th	H	T	U
2	0	0	0

➤ 2000

Th	H	T	U
3	0	0	0

➤ 3000

Th	H	T	U
4	0	0	0

➤ 4000

Th	H	T	U
5	0	0	0

➤ 5000

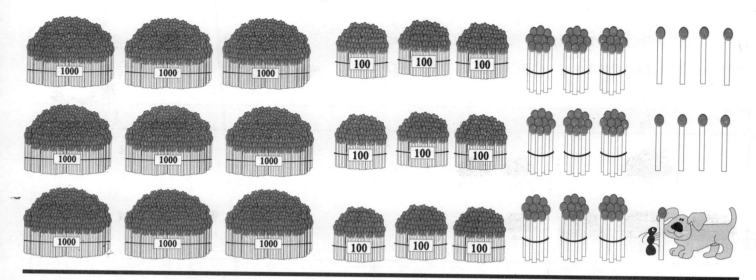

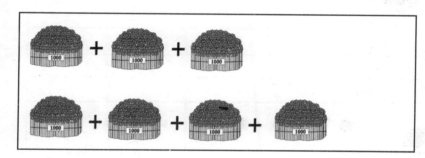

Th	H	T	U
6	0	0	0

➤ **6000**

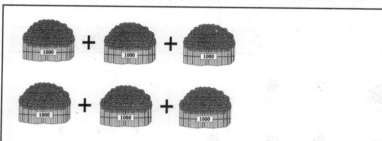

Th	H	T	U
7	0	0	0

➤ **7000**

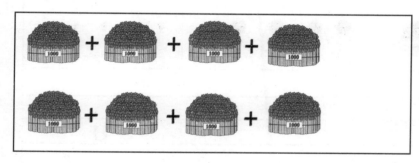

Th	H	T	U
8	0	0	0

➤ **8000**

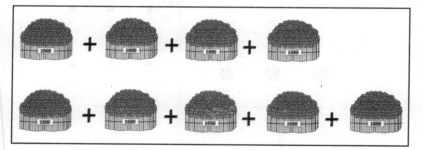

Th	H	T	U
9	0	0	0

➤ **9000**

Look at each **picture** and write the correct **numeral** in each **empty space**.

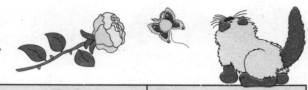

Th	H	T	U

Th	H	T	U

Th	H	T	U

Th	H	T	U

Let's know more about Thousands, Hundreds, Tens and Units.

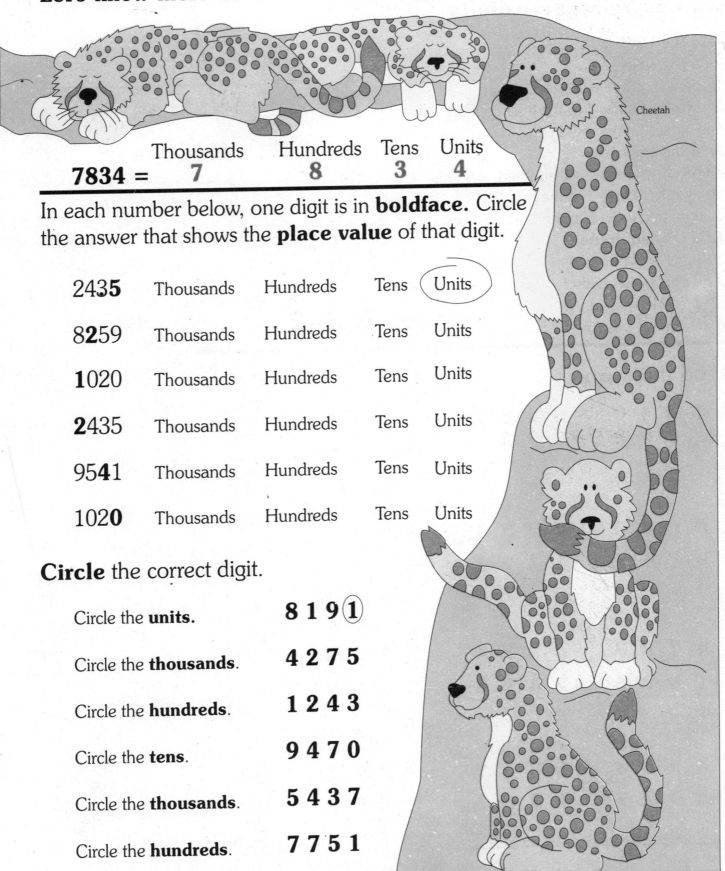

	Thousands	Hundreds	Tens	Units
7834 =	7	8	3	4

In each number below, one digit is in **boldface.** Circle the answer that shows the **place value** of that digit.

243**5**	Thousands	Hundreds	Tens	(Units)
8**2**59	Thousands	Hundreds	Tens	Units
1020	Thousands	Hundreds	Tens	Units
2435	Thousands	Hundreds	Tens	Units
95**4**1	Thousands	Hundreds	Tens	Units
102**0**	Thousands	Hundreds	Tens	Units

Circle the correct digit.

Circle the **units**.   8 1 9 ①

Circle the **thousands**.   4 2 7 5

Circle the **hundreds**.   1 2 4 3

Circle the **tens**.   9 4 7 0

Circle the **thousands**.   5 4 3 7

Circle the **hundreds**.   7 7 5 1

Cheetah

59

Adding Thousands, Hundreds, Tens and Units with carrying over digits

Add the Units :

7+5=12 units

12 units = 1 ten + 2 units

So, we shall carry 1 to the ten's column and write 2 in the unit's column

Add the tens :

8+6+ 1 = 15 tens =1 hundred + 5 tens

So, we shall carry 1 to the hundred's column and write 5 in the ten's column.

Add the hundreds :

2+4+ 1 = 7 hundreds.

Add the thousands :

7+2 = 9 thousands

therefore the **sum** = 9 7 5 2.

Thousands	Hundreds	Tens	Units
	1	1	
7	2	8	7
+ 2	4	6	5
9	7	5	2

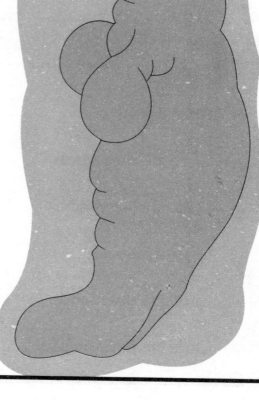

Find the sum.

```
   4 8 4 0        5 4 6 2        2 6 4 0
 + 1 0 2 3      + 2 9 2 3      + 3 1 7 3
 _____      _____      _____



   8 5 4 0        7 7 3 1        1 8 4 7
   + 4 8 2      + 1 2 7 3      + 6 2 5 9
 _____      _____      _____



   4 7 8 7        6 3 5 4        2 7 4 3
 + 1 8 9 6      + 2 4 9 8      + 5 1 8 9
 _____      _____      _____



   3 0 8 6        6 2 5 9        4 2 7 4
 + 5 0 2 7      + 1 3 6 2      + 3 8 9 9
 _____      _____      _____
```

5591 or **5** thousands,
5 hundreds, **9** tens
and **1** unit.

Thousands	Hundreds	Tens	Units
1		1	
3	**7**	**5**	**4**
+1	**8**	**3**	**7**
5	**5**	**9**	**1**

Find the **sum**.

```
   3 6 8        5 9 3        2 9 7        3 8 6
  +5 9 3       +6 6 8       +4 9 3       +8 5 7
  _____      _____      _____      _____
```

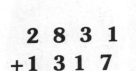

```
   3 3 3 3      9 0 5 4      3 2 8 9      8 7 2 1
   + 7 7 7      + 8 5 7     +1 9 3 1     +1 1 8 9
  _____    _____    _____    _____
```

```
   5 4 8 1      3 2 1 5      6 1 8 9      4 3 2 3
  +2 9 2 6     +2 3 5 8     +1 9 7 3     +1 6 5 3
  _____    _____    _____    _____
```

```
   2 8 3 1      2 9 2 6      1 2 5 5      1 9 7 3
  +1 3 1 7     +6 5 3 1     +2 9 2 6     +3 2 1 5
  _____    _____    _____    _____
```

```
   2 8 2 5      1 5 7 8      4 1 7 8      3 9 1 7
  +1 5 8 8     +5 2 6 3     +3 9 1 7     +1 4 2 0
  _____    _____    _____    _____
```

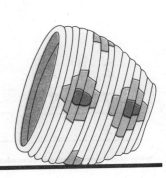

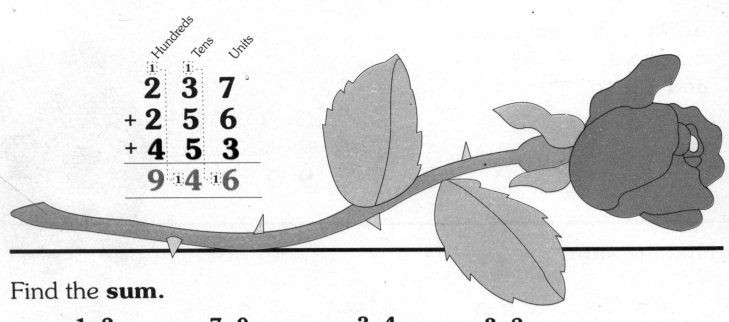

```
Hundreds  Tens  Units
  1     1
  2     3     7
+ 2     5     6
+ 4     5     3
  9     4     6
```

Find the **sum.**

```
   1 2        7 0        3 4        3 2
 + 5 6      + 1 9      + 5 9      + 1 6
 + 9 4      + 3 1      + 4 6      + 7 8
_____    _____    _____    _____


 1 0 5      3 9 2      1 1 6 2    1 3 2 2
+3 4 7     +7 4 7     +6 3 9 2   +7 4 1 1
+5 5 5     +7 4 1     +2 1 1 8   +1 0 7 8
_____    _____    _____  _____
```

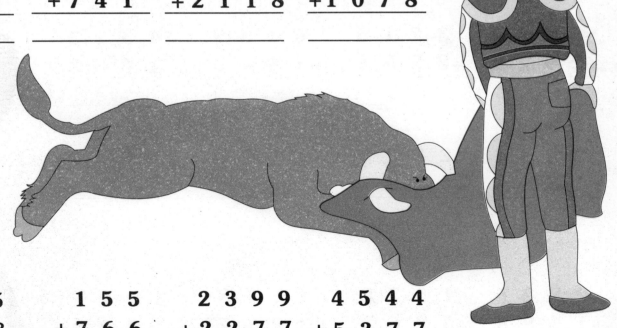

```
 2 4 5      1 5 5      2 3 9 9    4 5 4 4
+7 3 8     +7 6 6     +2 2 7 7   +5 3 7 7
_____    _____    _____  _____
```

Subtracting Thousands, Hundreds, Tens and Units with borrowing digits

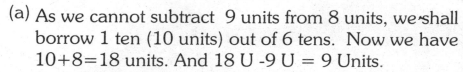

$$\begin{array}{r} {\scriptstyle 3\ \ 1\ \ 5} \\ 4\ \ \cancel{2}\ \ \cancel{6}\ \ 8 \\ -2\ \ 7\ \ 8\ \ 9 \\ \hline 1\ \ 4\ \ 7\ \ 9 \end{array}$$

(a) As we cannot subtract 9 units from 8 units, we shall borrow 1 ten (10 units) out of 6 tens. Now we have 10+8=18 units. And 18 U -9 U = 9 Units.

(b) We have 5 tens left. As we cannot subtract 8 tens from 5 tens, we shall borrow 1 hundred (10 tens) out of 2 hundreds. Now we have 10+5 =15 tens. And 15 tens - 8 tens = 7 Tens.

(c) We have 1 hundred left. As we cannot subtract 7 hundreds from 1 hundred, we shall borrow 1 thousand (10 hundreds) out of 4 thousands. Now we have 10+1 = 11 hundreds. And 11 h - 7 h = 4 Hundreds.

(d) We have 3 thousands left. 3 th - 2 th = 1 Thousand. Therefore Remainder = 1479.

Popocatepeti Volcano

Find the **remainder.**

$$\begin{array}{r} 8\ 7\ 9\ 2 \\ -6\ 5\ 8\ 7 \\ \hline \end{array} \qquad \begin{array}{r} 4\ 2\ 9\ 2 \\ -1\ 5\ 5\ 6 \\ \hline \end{array} \qquad \begin{array}{r} 6\ 7\ 5\ 3 \\ -2\ 5\ 7\ 5 \\ \hline \end{array} \qquad \begin{array}{r} 9\ 8\ 4\ 2 \\ -6\ 7\ 5\ 3 \\ \hline \end{array}$$

$$\begin{array}{r} 7\ 8\ 6\ 5 \\ -6\ 5\ 8\ 6 \\ \hline \end{array} \qquad \begin{array}{r} 7\ 8\ 8\ 5 \\ -4\ 7\ 4\ 1 \\ \hline \end{array} \qquad \begin{array}{r} 6\ 3\ 3\ 1 \\ -5\ 6\ 1\ 8 \\ \hline \end{array} \qquad \begin{array}{r} 4\ 6\ 8\ 2 \\ -2\ 7\ 7\ 4 \\ \hline \end{array}$$

Find the **remainder.**

$$
\begin{array}{r} 2\ 0\ 4 \\ -1\ 1\ 7 \\ \hline \end{array}
\qquad
\begin{array}{r} 4\ 0\ 8 \\ -\ 2\ 9 \\ \hline \end{array}
\qquad
\begin{array}{r} 8\ 0\ 0 \\ -5\ 2\ 9 \\ \hline \end{array}
$$

$$
\begin{array}{r} 6\ 7\ 0\ 0 \\ -\ 6\ 6\ 1 \\ \hline \end{array}
\qquad
\begin{array}{r} 6\ 0\ 0\ 0 \\ -1\ 2\ 7\ 8 \\ \hline \end{array}
\qquad
\begin{array}{r} 5\ 0\ 0\ 2 \\ -\ 4\ 4\ 3 \\ \hline \end{array}
$$

$$
\begin{array}{r} 2\ 7\ 2\ 1 \\ -1\ 0\ 7\ 0 \\ \hline \end{array}
\qquad
\begin{array}{r} 5\ 6\ 8\ 0 \\ -2\ 3\ 7\ 0 \\ \hline \end{array}
\qquad
\begin{array}{r} 7\ 9\ 8\ 9 \\ -2\ 8\ 7\ 7 \\ \hline \end{array}
$$

$$
\begin{array}{r} 9\ 9\ 9\ 9 \\ -8\ 8\ 0\ 0 \\ \hline \end{array}
\qquad
\begin{array}{r} 4\ 5\ 6\ 0 \\ -2\ 9\ 6\ 0 \\ \hline \end{array}
\qquad
\begin{array}{r} 8\ 6\ 8\ 0 \\ -2\ 5\ 9\ 0 \\ \hline \end{array}
\qquad
\begin{array}{r} 9\ 8\ 4\ 2 \\ -6\ 7\ 5\ 3 \\ \hline \end{array}
$$

Find the **remainder**.

```
  6 6 6        7 7 9 3        9 0 6 8
- 5 8 9      - 3 8 9 6      - 8 7 5 9
_____    _____    _____
```

```
  8 9 0        8 8 8 0        9 2 5 0
- 4 0 5      - 7 9 8 9      - 6 4 9 0
_____    _____    _____
```

```
  7 3 6        8 1 2 7        7 1 9 4
- 3 4 9      -   6 7 5      - 1 8 5 6
_____    _____    _____
```

```
  3 4 0        6 3 5 4        3 4 4 7
-   9 3      - 5 8 8 8      - 1 2 9 9
_____    _____    _____
```

```
  4 2 5 3      9 8 7 6        1 6 2 3
- 2 4 4 4    - 3 8 7 7      -   7 6 6
_____   _____    _____
```

```
  7 5 6 1      6 2 7 6        1 7 8 4
- 2 6 5 4    -   5 5 9      -   7 9 5
_____   _____    _____
```

Addition and Subtraction Practice - I

Find the **Sum**.

```
  2 6 8 5        4 0 6 5        8 0 6 5
+ 4 6 6 5      + 3 0 9 5      + 1 0 9 5
_____      _____      _____


  2 3 0 4        1 0 8 0        3 0 5 0
+ 6 9 0 6      +   2 9 0      + 2 9 5 0
_____      _____      _____


  2 8 6 0        2 9 5 6
+   8 9 0      + 3 0 6 7
_____      _____
```

Find the **remainder**.

```
  9 6 5 0        5 8 9 0        2 6 8 9
- 2 9 6 0      - 2 9 8 0      -   1 0 9
_____      _____      _____


  9 0 9 0        2 0 8 9        6 8 6 0
- 1 0 9 9      - 1 0 9 8      - 5 9 6 0
_____      _____      _____


  6 7 9 6        2 3 4 5        3 8 9 0
- 5 4 6 9      -   2 9 0      - 2 7 6 6
_____      _____      _____
```

Yapok

Addition and Subtraction Practice - II

Put a **cross (✗)** on each **incorrect answer.**

```
   5 0 6 0          3 8 4 0
 - 2 9 8 0        + 2 5 6 7
 ─────────        ─────────
   3 0 9 0          5 4 1 7
```

```
   2 9 8 0          2 9 6 5
 - 1 0 6 0        + 3 6 8 7
 ─────────        ─────────
   1 9 2 0          6 6 5 2
```

```
   9 8 6 5          2 5 6 0          8 0 6 0          5 0 6 0
 - 2 9 6 0        + 3 9 7 0        - 2 9 6 0        + 2 9 6 0
 ─────────        ─────────        ─────────        ─────────
   7 9 0 5          6 3 9 0          6 1 0 0          3 1 0 0
```

```
   4 0 7 9          9 0 8 9          7 0 6 5          6 0 8 9
 - 3 0 8 9        - 2 9 6 5        - 5 9 6 0        + 2 9 6 5
 ─────────        ─────────        ─────────        ─────────
   1 0 9 0          7 1 2 4          1 1 0 5          8 0 4 4
```

```
   2 0 6 8          2 4 3 2          5 0 6 6          9 9 9 9
 + 7 2 6 9        + 4 8 6 5        - 4 5 9 8        - 7 6 8 2
 ─────────        ─────────        ─────────        ─────────
   9 3 3 7          7 2 9 7          1 5 6 8          2 3 1 7
```

```
   5 8 9 7          2 5 6 8          7 8 9 6          3 8 9 6
 + 2 4 5 9        + 3 9 8 9        - 2 4 6 9        + 4 4 3 2
 ─────────        ─────────        ─────────        ─────────
   7 3 5 6          6 5 5 7          4 4 2 7          8 3 2 8
```

	Th	H	T	U
2 6 8 6 =	2	6	8	6

So, the numeral **2686** contains **2** thousands **(2000)** + six hundreds **(600)** + **8** tens **(80)** + **6** units **(6)**.

Or

$2000 + 600 + 80 + 6 = 2686$.

Now **read** and **write** the following **numerals** :

	Th	H	T	U
8 6 9 6				
6 0 0 0				
2 6 5 9				
5 0 7 8				
7 7 6 0				
8 8 5 0				
9 9 9 9				
2 5 6 9				
9 0 8 9				
5 4 6 7				

Indian Python

Words to Numerals

Three **thousands** six **hundreds** eight **tens** and six **units**.

Th	H	T	U

3 6 8 6 = 3 6 8 6

Make numerals from the following :

Three thousands seven hundreds six tens five units = __3 7 6 5__

Two thousand zero hundred seven tens two units = _____

Nine thousands six hundreds five tens zero unit = _____

Five thousands four hundreds three tens two units = _____

Four thousands one hundred three tens one unit = _____

One thousand nine hundreds eight tens seven units = _____

Six thousands three hundreds one ten two units = _____

Eight thousands nine hundreds three tens five units = _____

Three thousands one hundred two tens seven units = _____

Seven thousands six hundreds seven tens one unit = _____

Brazilian Tapir

	Th	H	T	U
3 6 8 5 =	3	6	8	5

Three thousand six hundred and eighty-five = 3 6 8 5

Five thousand two hundred and sixty-four = _____

Nine thousand two hundred and seventy-four = _____

Six thousand one hundred and fifty-four = _____

Eight thousand seven hundred and thirty-four = _____

Write in words

5 7 6 1 = Five thousand seven hundred and sixty-one.

8 6 4 6 = _____

9 2 2 1 = _____

6 5 2 0 = _____

8 7 4 6 = _____

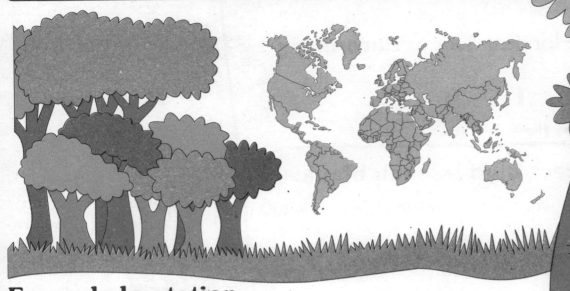

Expanded notation

$$8\ 2\ 6\ 8 = 8000 + 200 + 60 + 8$$

Or

In words :

$8\ 2\ 6\ 8 = 8$ thousands $+\ 2$ hundreds $+\ 6$ tens $+\ 8$ units

---

Break up the following **numerals** into **thousands, hundreds, tens** and **units :**

4 3 9 1   4000 + 300 + 90 + 1

8 2 7 5   _____

1 2 0 0   _____

5 6 8 0   _____

9 5 6 0   _____

Write the numerals in **expanded notation** using words.

2 9 5 5   *2 thousands + 9 hundreds + 5 tens + 5 units*

4 5 8 2   _____

1 0 2 3   _____

5 6 8 0   _____

7 8 8 0   _____

The **Volga,** the longest river in **Europe,** is **2194** miles.

2	1	9	4
Thousands	Hundreds	Tens	Units

Write the correct digit in each blank.

The **Amazon**, the world's second longest river, is **4000** miles.

_____	_____	_____	_____
Thousands	Hundreds	Tens	Units

The **Nile**, the longest river in the world, is **4145** miles.

_____	_____	_____	_____
Thousands	Hundreds	Tens	Units

The **Ganges**, considered sacred by the Hindus, is **1540** miles.

_____	_____	_____	_____
Thousands	Hundreds	Tens	Units

Write each numeral in its **standard form**.

9000 + 700 + 20 + 5 (expanded form)
9725 (standard form)

7000 + 400 + 30 + 2 = _____

6000 + 300 + 40 + 1 = _____

2000 + 600 + 20 + 6 = _____

5000 + 800 + 90 + 3 = _____

8000 + 100 + 60 + 9 = _____

1000 + 90 + 5 = _____

Black Skimmer

Across

1. **2** hundreds + **6** tens + **8** units
3. 3 hundreds + 9 tens + 7 units
5. 4 thousands + 7 hundreds + 8 tens + 0 unit
7. Three thousand three hundred and thirty three
8. 200 less than 9235
9. Six hundred and twenty-two
11. 6 hundreds + 7 tens + 8 units
13. 500 less than 5890
15. 8 thousands + 1 hundred + 2 tens + 6 units
16. 70 more than 120
17. Two thousand five hundred and fifty

Check your **answers** with the **numbers** written below :

Down

1. 2 thousands + 9 hundreds + 5 tens + 9 units
2. Eight thousand four hundred and thirty-three
3. 2000 more than 1036
4. 7 thousands + 3 hundreds + 9 tens + 2 units
6. 1000 less than 8354
10. Two thousand five hundred and ninety-nine
11. 10 less than 695
12. 400 more than 422
14. 3 hundreds + 1 ten + 0 unit

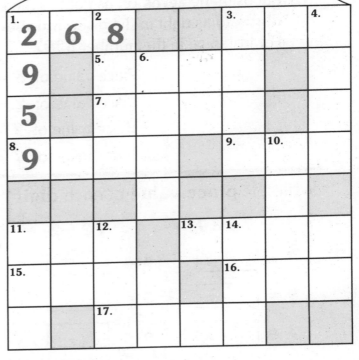

Galapagos Penguin

1. **2**	**6**	2. **8**			3.		4.
9		5.	6.				
5		7.					
8. **9**					9.	10.	
11.		12.		13.	14.		
15.					16.		
		17.					

73

Place Value

(a) Write the **digit** whose **place value** is to be found out.

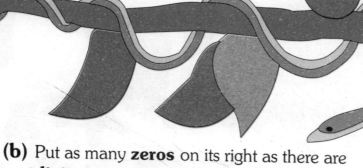

Vine Snake

Fruit Bat

(b) Put as many **zeros** on its right as there are **digits** to its right in the given **number**. For instance, in the number **3297**

Place value of **3** = **3000**

Place value of **2** = **200**

Place value of **9** = **90**

Place value of **7** = **7**

Write the **place value** of each **digit** in each **number**.

7 9 3 7

7 = ☐
9 = ☐
3 = ☐
7 = ☐

4 3 6 2

4 = ☐
3 = ☐
6 = ☐
2 = ☐

6 4 3 2

6 = ☐
4 = ☐
3 = ☐
2 = ☐

5 2 5 9

5 = ☐
2 = ☐
5 = ☐
9 = ☐

8 6 9 7

8 = ☐
6 = ☐
9 = ☐
7 = ☐

9 9 9 9

9 = ☐
9 = ☐
9 = ☐
9 = ☐

Across

1. **2** hundreds + **6** tens + **8** units

3. 3 hundreds + 9 tens + 7 units

5. 4 thousands + 7 hundreds + 8 tens + 0 unit

7. Three thousand three hundred and thirty three

8. 200 less than 9235

9. Six hundred and twenty-two

11. 6 hundreds + 7 tens + 8 units

13. 500 less than 5890

15. 8 thousands + 1 hundred + 2 tens + 6 units

16. 70 more than 120

17. Two thousand five hundred and fifty

Check your **answers** with the **numbers** written below :

Down

1. 2 thousands + 9 hundreds + 5 tens + 9 units

2. Eight thousand four hundred and thirty-three

3. 2000 more than 1036

4. 7 thousands + 3 hundreds + 9 tens + 2 units

6. 1000 less than 8354

10. Two thousand five hundred and ninety-nine

11. 10 less than 695

12. 400 more than 422

14. 3 hundreds + 1 ten + 0 unit

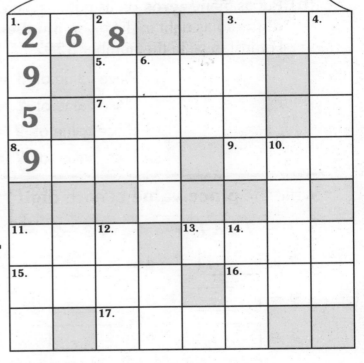

1. 2	6	2. 8			3.		4.
9		5.	6.				
5		7.					
8. 9					9.	10.	
11.		12.		13.	14.		
15.					16.		
		17.					

Galapagos Penguin

73

Place Value

(a) Write the **digit** whose **place value**
is to be found out.

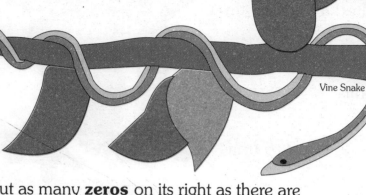

Vine Snake

Fruit Bat

(b) Put as many **zeros** on its right as there are
digits to its right in the given **number**.
For instance, in the number **3297**

Place value of **3** = **3000**

Place value of **2** = **200**

Place value of **9** =   **90**

Place value of **7** =   **7**

Write the **place value** of each **digit** in each **number**.

7 9 3 7

7 = [ ]
9 = [ ]
3 = [ ]
7 = [ ]

4 3 6 2

4 = [ ]
3 = [ ]
6 = [ ]
2 = [ ]

6 4 3 2

6 = [ ]
4 = [ ]
3 = [ ]
2 = [ ]

5 2 5 9

5 = [ ]
2 = [ ]
5 = [ ]
9 = [ ]

8 6 9 7

8 = [ ]
6 = [ ]
9 = [ ]
7 = [ ]

9 9 9 9

9 = [ ]
9 = [ ]
9 = [ ]
9 = [ ]

Write each set of **numerals** in order from the
least to the **greatest**.

7937, 780, 80, 5 ___ ___ ___ ___

460, 2560, 4, 56 ___ ___ ___ ___

3257, 555, 40, 2 ___ ___ ___ ___

50, 8, 670, 3492 ___ ___ ___ ___

6, 2080, 50, 920 ___ ___ ___ ___

920, 4060, 22, 9 ___ ___ ___ ___

5069, 28, 9, 659 ___ ___ ___ ___

Fill up the empty box.

	in 5689	in 6598	in 8965	in 9856
Place value of **9**				
Place value of **8**				
Place value of **6**				
Place value of **5**				

Table of 11

1 × 11 = __11__
2 × 11 = __22__
3 × 11 = __33__
4 × 11 = __44__
5 × 11 = __55__
6 × 11 = __66__
7 × 11 = __77__
8 × 11 = __88__
9 × 11 = __99__
10 × 11 = __110__

Table of 12

1 × 12 = __12__
2 × 12 = __24__
3 × 12 = __36__
4 × 12 = __48__
5 × 12 = __60__
6 × 12 = __72__
7 × 12 = __84__
8 × 12 = __96__
9 × 12 = __108__
10 × 12 = __120__

Table of 13

1 × 13 = __13__
2 × 13 = __26__
3 × 13 = __39__
4 × 13 = __52__
5 × 13 = __65__
6 × 13 = __78__
7 × 13 = __91__
8 × 13 = __104__
9 × 13 = __117__
10 × 13 = __130__

Table of 14

1 × 14 = __14__
2 × 14 = __28__
3 × 14 = __42__
4 × 14 = __56__
5 × 14 = __70__
6 × 14 = __84__
7 × 14 = __98__
8 × 14 = __112__
9 × 14 = __126__
10 × 14 = __140__

Table of 15

1 × 15 = __15__
2 × 15 = __30__
3 × 15 = __45__
4 × 15 = __60__
5 × 15 = __75__
6 × 15 = __90__
7 × 15 = __105__
8 × 15 = __120__
9 × 15 = __135__
10 × 15 = __150__

Jumping Spider

Table of 16

1 × 16 = __16__
2 × 16 = __32__
3 × 16 = __48__
4 × 16 = __64__
5 × 16 = __80__
6 × 16 = __96__
7 × 16 = __112__
8 × 16 = __128__
9 × 16 = __144__
10 × 16 = __160__

Table of 17

1 × 17 = __17__
2 × 17 = __34__
3 × 17 = __51__
4 × 17 = __68__
5 × 17 = __85__
6 × 17 = __102__
7 × 17 = __119__
8 × 17 = __136__
9 × 17 = __153__
10 × 17 = __170__

Barbary Ape

Table of 18

1 × 18 = __18__
2 × 18 = __36__
3 × 18 = __54__
4 × 18 = __72__
5 × 18 = __90__
6 × 18 = __108__
7 × 18 = __126__
8 × 18 = __144__
9 × 18 = __164__
10 × 18 = __180__

Table of 19

1 × 19 = __19__
2 × 19 = __38__
3 × 19 = __57__
4 × 19 = __76__
5 × 19 = __95__
6 × 19 = __114__
7 × 19 = __133__
8 × 19 = __152__
9 × 19 = __171__
10 × 19 = __190__

Table of 20

1 × 20 = __20__
2 × 20 = __40__
3 × 20 = __60__
4 × 20 = __80__
5 × 20 = __100__
6 × 20 = __120__
7 × 20 = __140__
8 × 20 = __160__
9 × 20 = __180__
10 × 20 = __200__

Multiplication without carrying over digits

T	U
3	4
×	2
6	8

H	T	U
2	3	1
×		2
4	6	2

Th	H	T	U
2	3	1	2
×			2
4	6	2	4

I'm out of here !

Robin

Find the product.

T	U
2	3
×	2

H	T	U
1	1	4
×		2

Th	H	T	U
4	3	3	2
×			2

4	3
×	2

3	0	2
×		3

3	2	0	1
×			3

2	2
×	2

2	3	3
×		3

1	1	1	1
×			8

3	3
×	2

2	1	2
×		4

2	0	2	1
×			4

2	1
×	3

2	3	0
×		4

3	2	1	4
×			2

Multiplication with carrying over digits

(A) Multiply the units

```
H  T  U
3  6  4
      ↑
   ×  4
─────────
      6
```

$4 \times 4 = 16$ units

$16 = \textbf{1 ten}$ and 6 units

(B) Multiply the tens

```
H  T  U
3  6  4
   ↖
   ×  4
─────────
   5  6
```

$4 \times 6 = 24$ tens

24 tens $+ \textbf{1 ten} = 25$ tens

25 tens $= \textbf{2 hundreds}$ and 5 tens

(C) Multiply the hundreds

```
Th  H  T  U
    3  6  4
      ↖
    ×     4
──────────────
 1  4  5  6
```

$4 \times 3 = \textbf{12 hundreds}$

12 hundreds $+ \textbf{2 hundreds} = 14$ hundreds

Flamingo

Find the product.

```
  3 0 2        4 0 2        6 8 2
  ×   3        ×   5        ×   3
_____      _____     _____


  1 8 2        5 0 8        7 8 9
  ×   2        ×   2        ×   2
_____      _____     _____


  2 0 1        3 2 0        3 0 1
  ×   5        ×   6        ×   8
_____      _____     _____
```

Multiplying by Multiples of Ten

Big Brown Bat

Th	H	T	U
		2	0
	x	6	0
1	2	0	0

When we **multiply** a number by a **multiple** of ten (**10, 20, 30, 40, 50, 60 etc.**), first multiply the numbers without zeros. Here we have two numbers — **20** & **60** . Their **product** without their zeros is **2 x 6 = 12**. Now **add** the two zeros to the right of the **product** so obtained, i.e **1200**.

Mouse-Eared Bat

Find the product.

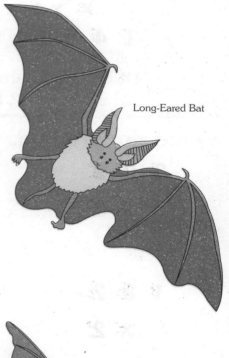

Long-Eared Bat

$$
\begin{array}{r} 30 \\ \times 40 \\ \hline \end{array}
\qquad
\begin{array}{r} 50 \\ \times 50 \\ \hline \end{array}
\qquad
\begin{array}{r} 80 \\ \times 70 \\ \hline \end{array}
$$

$$
\begin{array}{r} 40 \\ \times 90 \\ \hline \end{array}
\qquad
\begin{array}{r} 60 \\ \times 30 \\ \hline \end{array}
\qquad
\begin{array}{r} 20 \\ \times 30 \\ \hline \end{array}
$$

$$
\begin{array}{r} 80 \\ \times 20 \\ \hline \end{array}
\qquad
\begin{array}{r} 40 \\ \times 60 \\ \hline \end{array}
\qquad
\begin{array}{r} 40 \\ \times 50 \\ \hline \end{array}
$$

$$
\begin{array}{r} 30 \\ \times 50 \\ \hline \end{array}
\qquad
\begin{array}{r} 40 \\ \times 70 \\ \hline \end{array}
\qquad
\begin{array}{r} 80 \\ \times 90 \\ \hline \end{array}
$$

Free-Tailed bat

Multiplying a 2-digit number by a 2-digit number

```
  Th H T U
        5 4
    x   3 8
    ─────────
      4 3 2
    1 6 2 x
    ─────────
    2 0 5 2
    ─────────
```

(1) **Multiply** by the unit's digit **8** and write its **partial product** from below the unit's place.

(2) **Multiply** by the ten's digit **3** and write its **partial product** from below the ten's place.

(3) **Add** both the **partial products**. So, required product = **2052**.

Find the product

```
    3 1          4 6          8 6
  x 7 7        x 2 2        x 6 5
  ───────      ───────      ───────
```

```
    5 3          6 2          5 9
  x 4 4        x 2 5        x 2 5
  ───────      ───────      ───────
```

```
    5 5          9 1          8 7
  x 3 8        x 1 1        x 2 1
  ───────      ───────      ───────
```

Arrau River Turtle

```
    7 5          2 0          6 5          4 0
  x 1 5        x 1 2        x 2 5        x 2 2
  ───────      ───────      ───────      ───────
```

Multiplying a 3-digit number by a 2-digit number

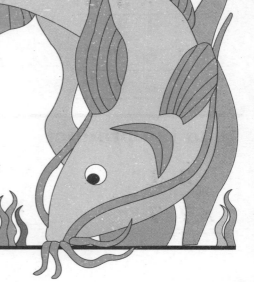

Blue Catfish

Th	H	T	U
	3	2	4
	×	1	8
2	5	9	2
3	2	4	×
5	8	3	2

(1) **Multiply** by the unit's digit **8** and write its **partial product** from below the unit's place.

(2) **Multiply** by the ten's digit **1** and write its **partial product** from below the ten's place.

(3) **Add** both the **partial products**. So, required product = **5832**

Find the product.

2 7 3	2 6 2	2 4 4	2 3 7
× 2 1	× 3 2	× 2 2	× 2 4

2 2 6	3 2 4	1 0 5	7 6 5
× 4 3	× 4 7	× 9 2	× 7 2

1 2 6	2 3 4	5 0 1	9 2 8
× 5 3	× 7 4	× 8 2	× 5 1

Crayfish

Practice - I

Find the product.

3 6 × 5	7 1 × 8	1 9 × 9	2 9 × 8
5 0 × 6	5 8 × 4	8 7 × 7	5 7 × 5
2 5 × 3	7 5 × 9	4 4 × 9	7 4 × 6
6 2 × 3	7 4 × 5	5 9 × 8	4 2 × 4
2 8 × 8	4 4 × 5	3 8 × 6	5 6 × 9
9 2 × 7	4 9 × 6		

Practice - II

Find each product in the **number search** below. Go **horizontally**, **vertically** and **diagonally** to search for each product.

```
  1 2 6          4 7 2          9 7 5
  x   4          x   2          x   4
  -----          -----          -----
  5 0 4

  1 3 4          8 1 3          1 4 4
  x   7          x   3          x   8
  -----          -----          -----


  1 3 5          2 9 2
  x   2          x   5
  -----          -----


  2 2 4
  x   9
  -----
```

Sulphur-Crested
Cockatoo

2	1	1	5	2	9
5	0	4	4	7	4
3	3	1	9	0	4
9	0	8	6	4	2
0	2	4	3	9	7
0	1	4	9	3	8

Number search

11 | DIVISION

  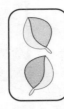

We can write a division problem as below:

$$6 \div 3 = 2$$

6 in all, divided by **3** sets= **2** in each set

Or $6 \div 2 = 3$

6 in all, divided by **2** in each set = **3** sets

There are **3** sets of **2** in **6**.

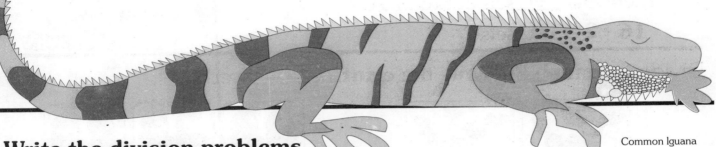

Common Iguana

Write the division problems.

_____ ÷ _____ = _____ in each set   _____ ÷ _____ = _____ in each set

_____ ÷ _____ = _____ sets   _____ ÷ _____ = _____ sets

_____ ÷ _____ = _____ in each set   _____ ÷ _____ = _____ in each set

_____ ÷ _____ = _____ sets   _____ ÷ _____ = _____ sets

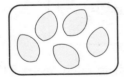    

_____ ÷ _____ = _____ in each set   _____ ÷ _____ = _____ in each set

_____ ÷ _____ = _____ sets   _____ ÷ _____ = _____ sets

85

Dividing by 2

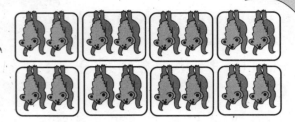

There are __8__ sets of two in **16**.

16 ÷ 2 =__8__ sets

Townsend's
Big-eared Bat

Divide the numbers. Write the **quotient** (answer).

There are _____ sets of two in **4**.

4 ÷ 2 =_____ sets

There are _____ sets of two in 6.

6 ÷ 2 =_____ sets

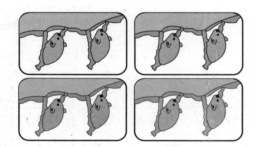

There are _____ sets of two in 8.

8 ÷ 2 =_____ sets

There are _____ sets of two in 10.

10 ÷ 2 =_____ sets

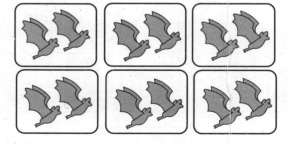

There are _____ sets of two in 12.

12 ÷ 2 =_____ sets

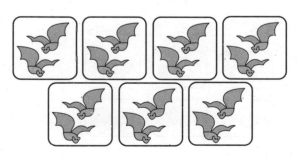

There are _____ sets of two in 14.

14 ÷ 2 =_____ sets

Dividing by 3

There are ___8___ sets of three in **24**.

24 ÷ 3 = ___8___ sets

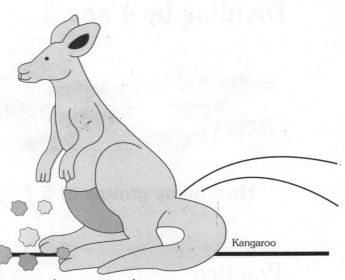

Kangaroo

Divide the numbers. Write the **quotient** (answer).

There are _____ sets of three in **6**.

6 ÷ 3 = _____ sets

There are _____ sets of three in **9**.

9 ÷ 3 = _____ sets

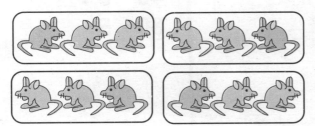

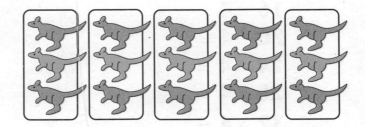

There are _____ sets of three in **12**.

12 ÷ 3 = _____ sets

There are _____ sets of three in **15**.

15 ÷ 3 = _____ sets

There are _____ sets of three in **18**.

18 ÷ 3 = _____ sets

There are _____ sets of three in **21**.

21 ÷ 3 = _____ sets

Dividing by 4 and 5

  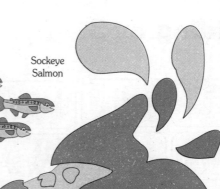

Sockeye Salmon

How many groups of 5 ? _____

Blue Whale

Practice

Divide the **numbers.**
Write the **quotient**.

$4 \div 2 =$ _____

$6 \div 3 =$ _____

$8 \div 4 =$ _____

$12 \div 4 =$ _____

$16 \div 4 =$ _____

$20 \div 4 =$ _____

$24 \div 4 =$ _____

$28 \div 4 =$ _____

$32 \div 4 =$ _____

$36 \div 4 =$ _____

$36 \div 4 =$ _____

$10 \div 2 =$ _____

$45 \div 5 =$ _____

$20 \div 5 =$ _____

$25 \div 5 =$ _____

$18 \div 6 =$ _____

$16 \div 4 =$ _____

$21 \div 3 =$ _____

$15 \div 5 =$ _____

$21 \div 7 =$ _____

$72 \div 9 =$ _____

$30 \div 5 =$ _____

$35 \div 5 =$ _____

$40 \div 5 =$ _____

$80 \div 5 =$ _____

$45 \div 5 =$ _____

$15 \div 5 =$ _____

$20 \div 2 =$ _____

$12 \div 3 =$ _____

$18 \div 2 =$ _____

$10 \div 5 =$ _____

$12 \div 2 =$ _____

$28 \div 4 =$ _____

$90 \div 9 =$ _____

Multiplication Helps Division

If we know our **multiplication tables** we can easily do **division**.

Here is a multiplication problem : $4 \times 3 = 12$

We can rewrite it as a division problem : $12 \div 3 = 4$

Or $12 \div 4 = 3$

Okapi

Write the division problem for each.

$8 \times 7 = 56$

$\underline{56} \div \underline{7} = \underline{8}$

$\underline{56} \div \underline{8} = \underline{7}$

$4 \times 9 = 36$

_____ ÷ _____ = _____

_____ ÷ _____ = _____

$5 \times 5 = 25$

_____ ÷ _____ = _____

_____ ÷ _____ = _____

$6 \times 7 = 42$

_____ ÷ _____ = _____

_____ ÷ _____ = _____

$3 \times 8 = 24$

_____ ÷ _____ = _____

_____ ÷ _____ = _____

$2 \times 7 = 14$

_____ ÷ _____ = _____

_____ ÷ _____ = _____

$7 \times 5 = 35$

_____ ÷ _____ = _____

_____ ÷ _____ = _____

$8 \times 9 = 72$

_____ ÷ _____ = _____

_____ ÷ _____ = _____

$4 \times 8 = 32$

_____ ÷ _____ = _____

_____ ÷ _____ = _____

$9 \times 5 = 45$

_____ ÷ _____ = _____

_____ ÷ _____ = _____

$4 \times 9 = 36$

_____ ÷ _____ = _____

_____ ÷ _____ = _____

$8 \times 5 = 40$

_____ ÷ _____ = _____

_____ ÷ _____ = _____

Solve each of the following **division** problems.
Write the **multiplication problem** that goes with
the **division problem**.

$18 \div 3 =$ ___6___ $6 \times 3 = 18$

$36 \div 9 =$ _____   _____

$54 \div 6 =$ _____   _____

$9 \div 3 =$ _____   _____

$28 \div 7 =$ _____   _____

$40 \div 10 =$ _____   _____

$88 \div 11 =$ _____   _____

$84 \div 12 =$ _____   _____

$15 \div 3 =$ _____   _____

$108 \div 12 =$ _____   _____

$60 \div 10 =$ _____   _____

$32 \div 4 =$ _____   _____

Giant Ahuehuete

Below are several Mexican objects. To solve the problems within the objects, **divide** each of the numbers by the number in the **centre**. Write your answer in the blank.

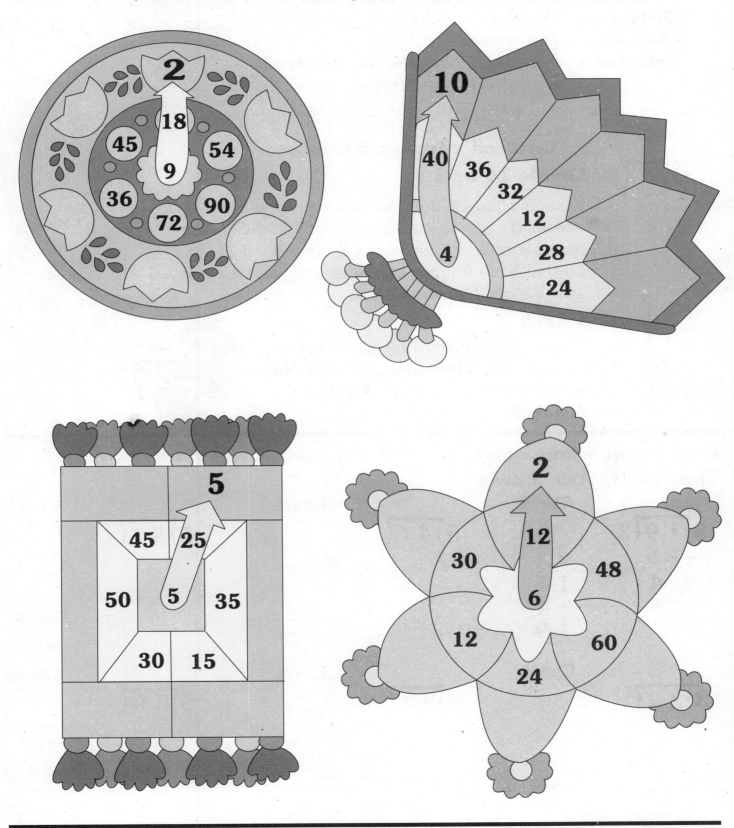

One-digit Quotient

We must know 4 words :

Dividend - The number that is being divided.
Divisor - The number that divides the dividend.
Quotient - The answer.
Remainder - What is left over after the **dividend** is divided by the **divisor**.

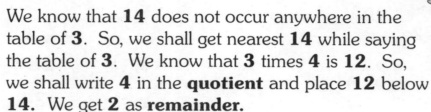

$$12 \div 3 = 4$$

Dividend ÷ **Divisor** = **Quotient**

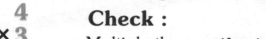

```
3)14(4
 -12
   2
```

Divide 14 by 3 :

We know that **14** does not occur anywhere in the table of **3**. So, we shall get nearest **14** while saying the table of **3**. We know that **3** times **4** is **12**. So, we shall write **4** in the **quotient** and place **12** below **14**. We get **2** as **remainder**.

```
   4
 × 3
  12
 + 2
  14
```

Check :

Multiply the **quotient** by the **divisor** and then add the **remainder** to the **product** so obtained. This will be equal to the **dividend**.

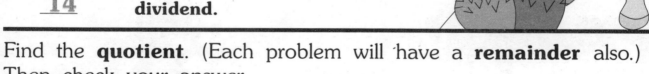

Find the **quotient**. (Each problem will have a **remainder** also.)
Then check your answer.

```
          Check              Check                 Check
5)19(3      5          5)46(                 5)81(
 -15      × 3                  ×                    ×
   4       15          ____                  ____
         + 4                  +                    +
          19           ____                  ____


          Check              Check                 Check
3)22(                 8)71(                 5)39(
          ×                  ×                    ×
____                 ____                  ____
         +                  +                    +
____                 ____                  ____
```

Two-Digit Quotient

```
5) 73 (14
   -5
    23
   -20
     3
```

(1) On **dividing 7** by **5**, we get **1** as **quotient** and **2** as **remainder**.

(2) Bringing down **3** and writing it with **2**, we get **23**. On **dividing 23** by **5**, we get 4 as **quotient** and **3** as **remainder**.

Hence **quotient** = **14**
Remainder = **3**

```
  14
 × 5
  70
 + 3
  73
```

Check :

Multiply the **quotient** (answer) by the **divisor** and then add the **remainder** to the product so obtained. This will be equal to the **dividend**.

Parnell's Mustached Bat

Vampair Bat

Find the **quotient**.

```
4) 9 1 (
```
Check
× ____
____
+ ____
____

```
6) 8 9 (
```
Check
× ____
____
+ ____
____

```
3) 7 7 (
```
Check
× ____
____
+ ____
____

```
7) 8 8 (
```
Check
× ____
____
+ ____
____

```
2) 6 3 (
```
Check
× ____
____
+ ____
____

```
5) 9 6 (
```
Check
× ____
____
+ ____
____

93

Three-digit Quotient

```
      Th H T U
    3)2958(986
     -27
      ‾‾‾‾
      25
     -24
      ‾‾‾‾
      18
     -18
      ‾‾‾‾
       0
```

As the left-most digit in the **dividend** is **2** and the **divisor** is **3**, we shall have to take **2** and **9** together.

(a) Say the table of **3** to reach **29**. We shall write **9** in the **quotient** and **27** under **29**. On **subtraction**, we get **2** as **remainder**.

(b) Bringing down **5**, we get **25**. Again say the table of **3** to reach **25**. We shall write **8** in the **quotient** and **24** under **25**. On **subtraction**, we get **1** as **remainder**.

(c) Bringing down **8**, we get **18**. Again say the table of **3** to reach **18**. We shall write **6** in the **quotient** and we get **0** as **remainder**. Hence **quotient = 986**, **remainder = 0**

Praying Mantis

Find the **quotient**.

4)5 2 1 2(Check
                  ×
                 ‾‾‾‾

4) 6 3 8(Check
                  ×
                 ‾‾‾‾

4) 9 3 6(Check
                  ×
                 ‾‾‾‾

4)2 1 0 5(Check
                  ×
                 ‾‾‾‾

4)4 8 5 2(Check
                  ×
                 ‾‾‾‾

4) 4 4 9(Check
                  ×
                 ‾‾‾‾

Jumping Spider

Divide taking two digits / three digits together

Th H T U

29) 2407 (83
  −232
  ─────
    87
  − 87
  ─────
     0

Here two digits taken together form **24** which is smaller than the **divisor 29**. So, we shall have to take three digits, i.e. **2, 4** and **0** together. They form **240**. Dividing it buy **29**, we shall write **8** in the **quotient** and **232** under **240**. On subtraction, we shall get **8** as **remainder**. Bringing down **7**, we get **87**. Dividing **87** by **29,** we shall write **3** in the **quotient** and **87** under **87**. On **subtraction,** we shall get **0** as **remainder.**

Striped Skunk

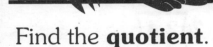

Find the **quotient**.

Check

29) 5 2 1 (× _____

Check

30) 2 0 7 0 (× _____

Check

30) 9 3 0 (× _____

Check

43) 6 2 0 0 (× _____

Check

60) 5 1 8 (× _____

Check

21) 6 2 5 (× _____

Division Review - I

Find the **quotient**.

144 ÷ 12 =   80 ÷ 10 =   72 ÷ 8 =

6)4 8(6)1 8(2)2 4(

99 ÷ 11 =   36 ÷ 9 =   63 ÷ 7 =

5)3 5(3)2 1(1)1 2(

132 ÷ 12 =   40 ÷ 10 =   16 ÷ 8 =

6)5 7(4)2 0(2)2 2(

Division Review - II

Koala

Find the **quotient**.

<table>
<tr><td>2⟌38⟍</td><td>Check
× ___
+ ___</td><td>6⟌189⟍</td><td>Check
× ___
+ ___</td><td>7⟌91⟍</td><td>Check
× ___
+ ___</td></tr>
<tr><td>5⟌209⟍</td><td>Check
× ___
+ ___</td><td>9⟌95⟍</td><td>Check
× ___
+ ___</td><td>3⟌53⟍</td><td>Check
× ___
+ ___</td></tr>
<tr><td>6⟌75⟍</td><td>Check
× ___
+ ___</td><td>5⟌298⟍</td><td>Check
× ___
+ ___</td><td>6⟌500⟍</td><td>Check
× ___
+ ___</td></tr>
</table>

12 | TELLING TIME

A **clock** has two **hands**. The **short-hand** shows the **hours** and the **long-hand** shows the **minutes**.

It is 2 o' clock
2:00

Read the **hour-hand** first and then read the **minute-hand**.
Write the **time** below each **clock**.

_____2_____ o'clock

2 : 00

_____ o'clock

____ : ____

_____ o'clock

____ : ____

_____ o'clock

____ : ____

_____ o'clock

____ : ____

_____ o'clock

____ : ____

Half Past

The **long-hand** tells the minutes. Here the **minute-hand** points to the **6.** The hour-hand is between **2** and **3**.

It is **half past 2**.

2:30

Read the **hour-hand** first and then read the **minute-hand**. Write the **time** below each **clock.**

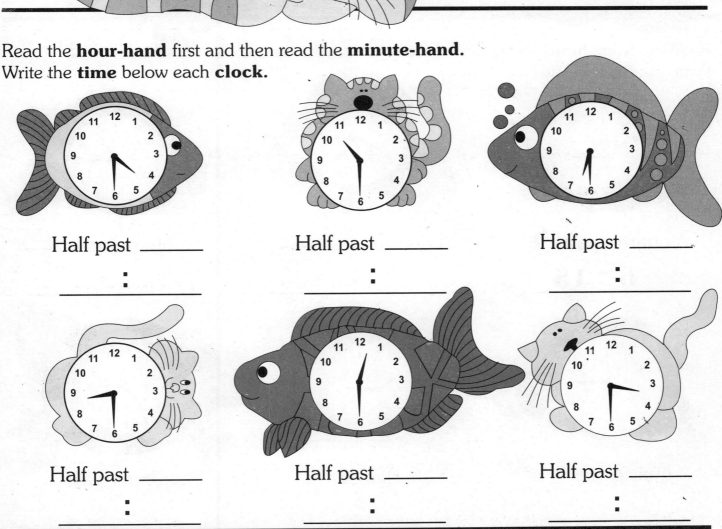

Half past _____

___ : ___

Half past _____

___ : ___

Half past _____

___ : ___

Half past _____

___ : ___

Half past _____

___ : ___

Half past _____

___ : ___

Quarter past

Here the **minute-hand** points to the **3**. The **hour-hand** is a little past **2:00**. It is a **quarter past** two.

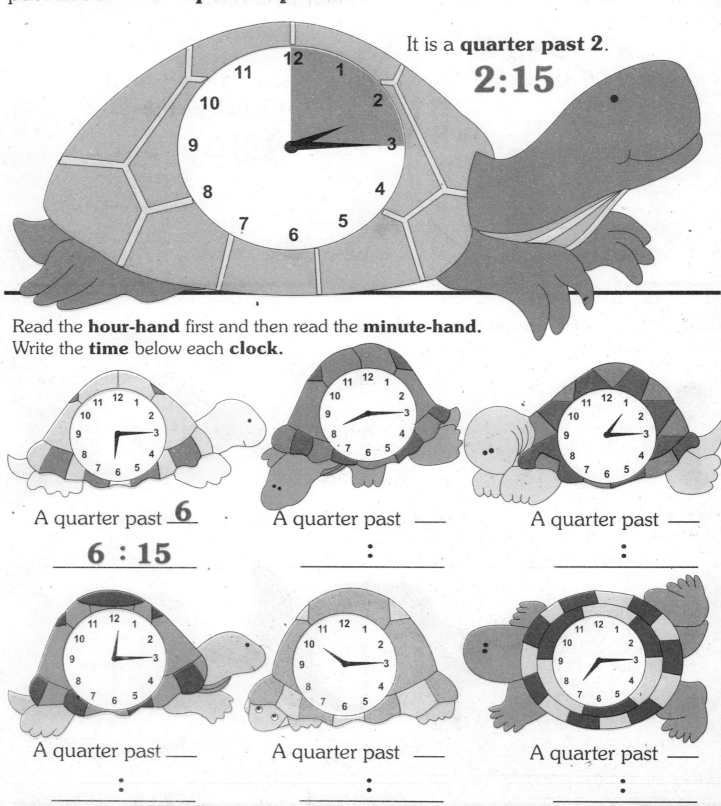

It is a **quarter past 2**.

2:15

Read the **hour-hand** first and then read the **minute-hand**. Write the **time** below each **clock**.

A quarter past __6__

__6 : 15__

A quarter past ____

___ : ___

A quarter past ____

___ : ___

A quarter past ____

___ : ___

A quarter past ____

___ : ___

A quarter past ____

___ : ___

Quarter to

Here the **minute-hand** points to the **9**.
The **hour-hand** is almost to the **3**.

It is a **quarter to 3**.

2:45

Read the **hour-hand** first and then read the **minute-hand**.
Write the **time** below each **clock**.

A quarter to __4__

3 : 45

A quarter to _____

___ : ___

A quarter to _____

___ : ___

A quarter to _____

___ : ___

A quarter to _____

___ : ___

A quarter to _____

___ : ___

Minutes

The **minute-hand** of a clock takes **5 minutes** to move from one number to the next. Count by fives. Start from **12**.

Write the **minutes** on each line.

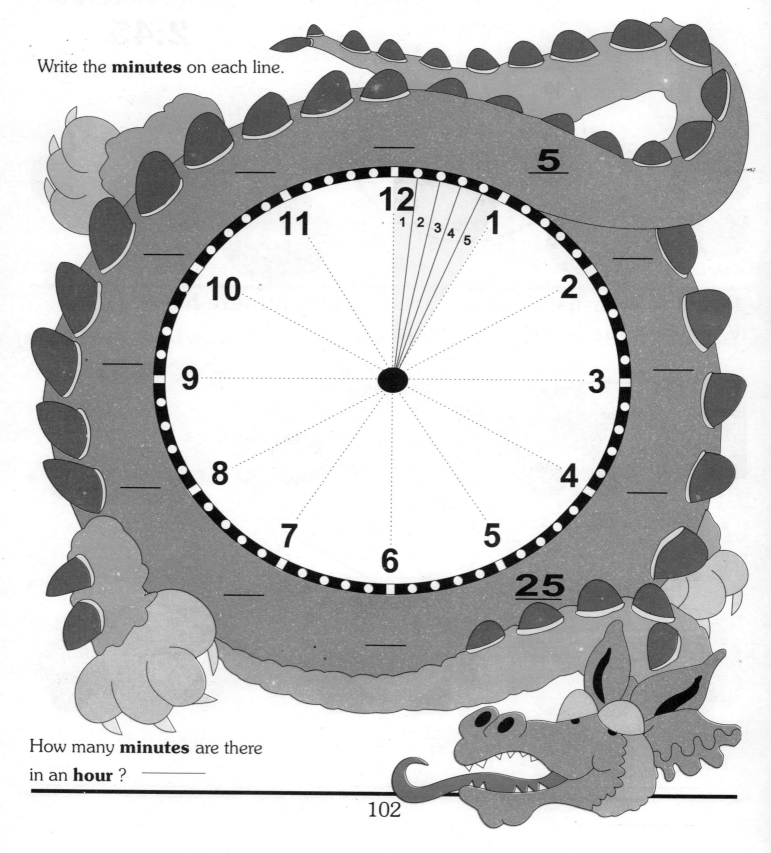

How many **minutes** are there in an **hour** ? _____

13 OUR CURRENCY

Front RUPEE 1 RUPEE 1997   **Back** INDIA INDIA ONE RUPEE

Front INDIA INDIA 2   **Back** INDIA 1997 NATIONAL INTERNATIONAL

Front RUPEES 5 RUPEES 1997   **Back** INDIA INDIA

Write the **amount** on the line.

Rs _____ **7**

Rs _____

It makes sense to count our rupees!

Rs _____

Rs _____

Can You Count these Coins ?

What is the **price** of each **toy** ? **Count** the **coins** below. Write the **amount** on the line.

__5__   __10__   __12__   __13__   __14__ Rs__15__

_____

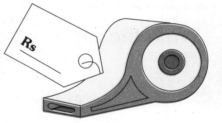

_____

_____

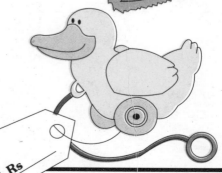

____   ____   ____   ____   ____

Write the **amount** on each line.
Is there enough **money** to pay for each item ?

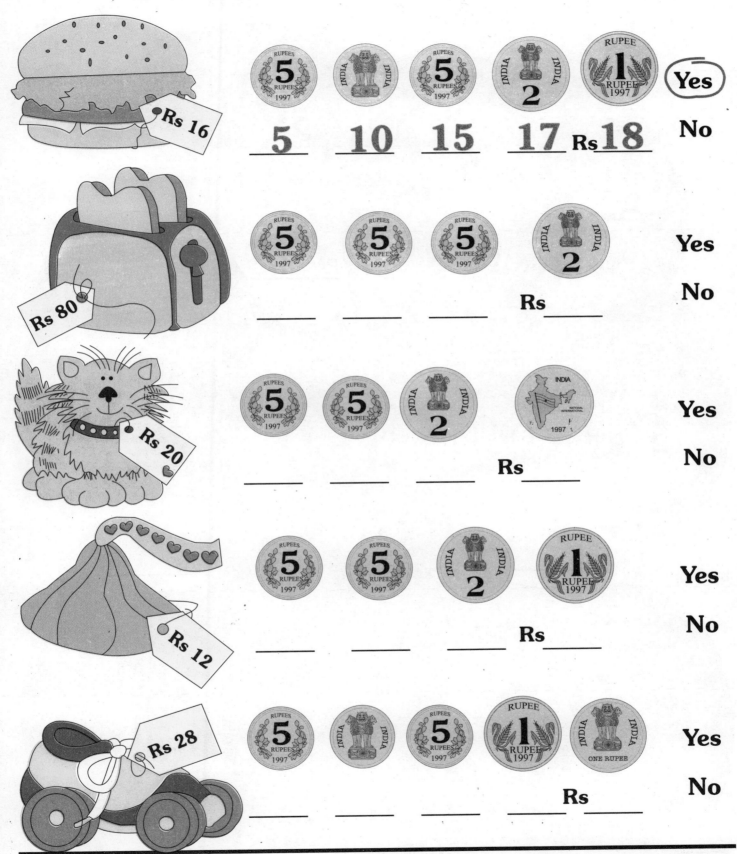

Rs 16

5   10   15   17   Rs 18

Yes

No

Rs 80

Yes

No

Rs _____

Rs 20

Yes

No

Rs _____

Rs 12

Yes

No

_____ _____ _____ Rs _____

Rs 28

Yes

No

_____ Rs _____

Count the coins in each group.
Write the amount on the line.

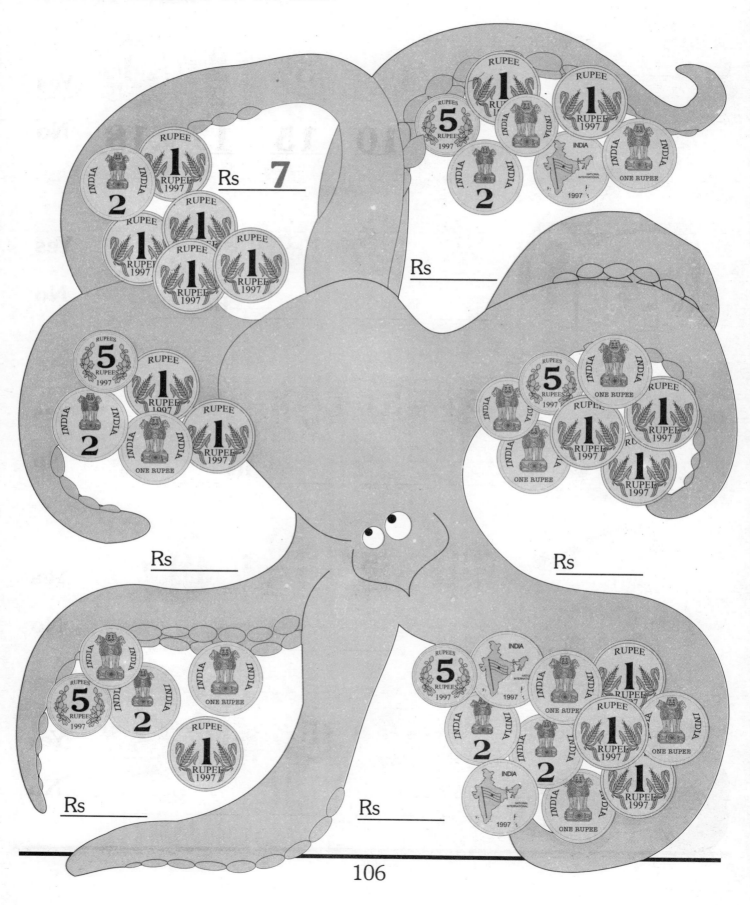

Rs ___7___

Rs _____

Rs _____

Rs _____

Rs _____

Rs _____

106

Going to the Store

How much does each item **cost** ?

   Rs **39**

   + Rs **28**

How much in all ?   Rs **67**

     Rs

     + Rs

How much in all ?   Rs

     Rs

     + Rs

How much in all ?   Rs

     Rs

   + Rs

How much in all ?   Rs

   Rs

     + Rs

How much in all ?   Rs

     Rs

   + Rs

How much in all ?   Rs

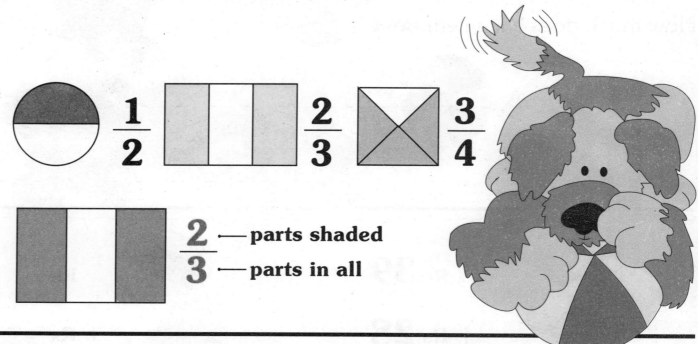

$$\frac{1}{2}$$ $$\frac{2}{3}$$ $$\frac{3}{4}$$

$$\frac{2}{3}$$ —— **parts shaded**

—— **parts in all**

Write the correct **fraction** for each **shaded object.**

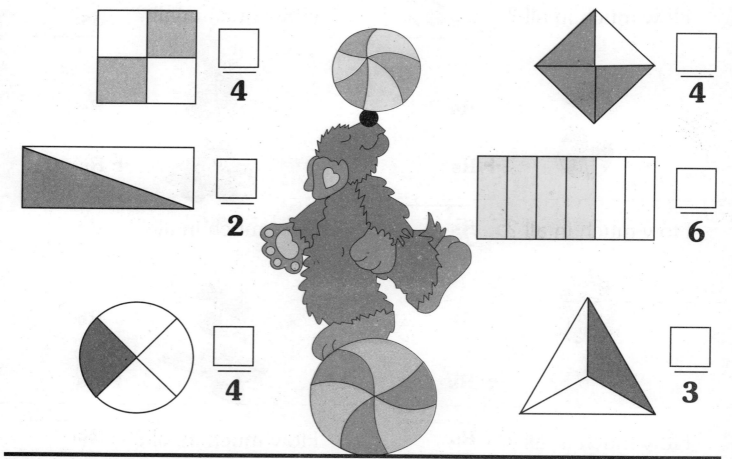

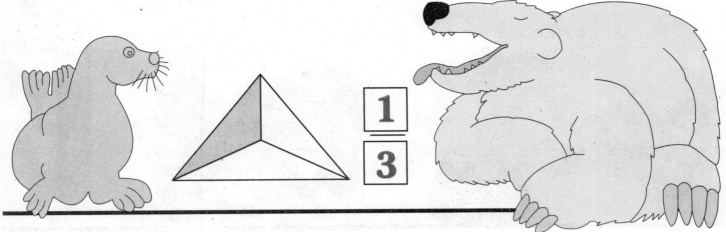

Colour the shape. Write the fraction
for each shape :

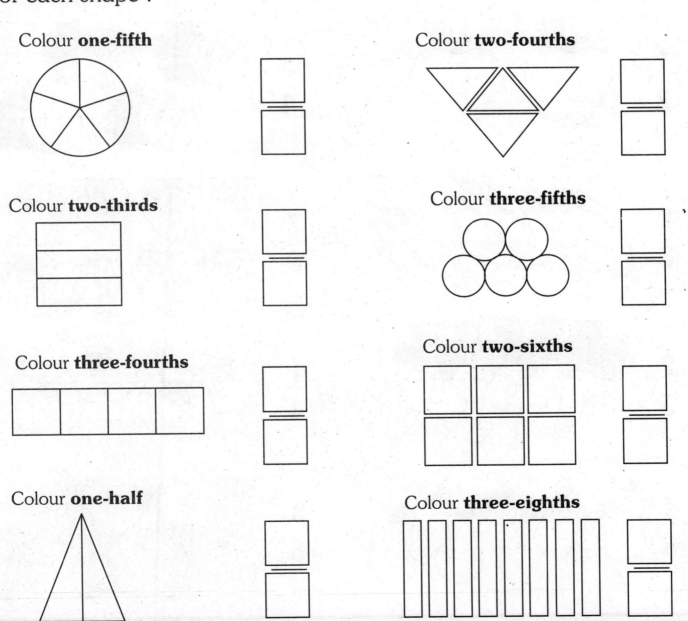

Colour **one-fifth**

Colour **two-fourths**

Colour **two-thirds**

Colour **three-fifths**

Colour **three-fourths**

Colour **two-sixths**

Colour **one-half**

Colour **three-eighths**

Colour the objects to show the fraction.

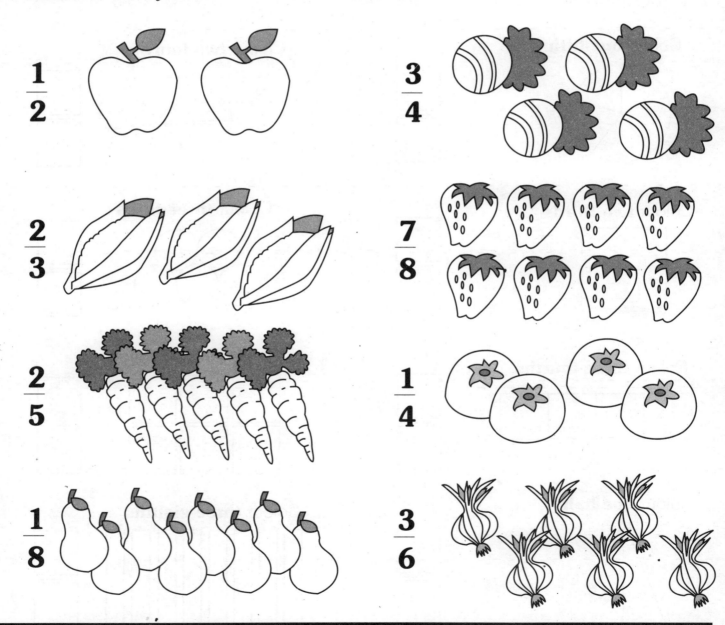

$\dfrac{1}{2}$

$\dfrac{2}{3}$

$\dfrac{2}{5}$

$\dfrac{1}{8}$

$\dfrac{3}{4}$

$\dfrac{7}{8}$

$\dfrac{1}{4}$

$\dfrac{3}{6}$

Circle the correct fraction.

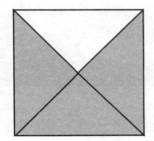

$\dfrac{3}{4}$ $\dfrac{1}{4}$ $\dfrac{2}{3}$

$\dfrac{3}{3}$ $\dfrac{1}{2}$ $\dfrac{1}{3}$

$\dfrac{1}{8}$ $\dfrac{7}{8}$ $\dfrac{3}{8}$

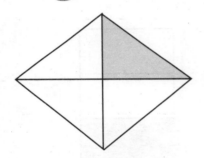

$\dfrac{1}{8}$ $\dfrac{2}{3}$ $\dfrac{1}{4}$

$\dfrac{1}{6}$ $\dfrac{1}{2}$ $\dfrac{2}{6}$

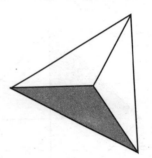

$\dfrac{1}{4}$ $\dfrac{1}{3}$ $\dfrac{1}{2}$

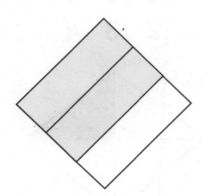

$\dfrac{1}{3}$ $\dfrac{2}{3}$ $\dfrac{1}{2}$

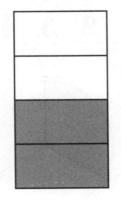

$\dfrac{3}{4}$ $\dfrac{1}{4}$ $\dfrac{2}{4}$

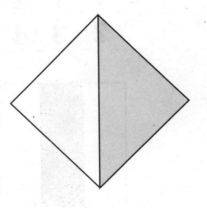

$\dfrac{1}{3}$ $\dfrac{1}{2}$ $\dfrac{3}{4}$

111

Circle the correct fraction.

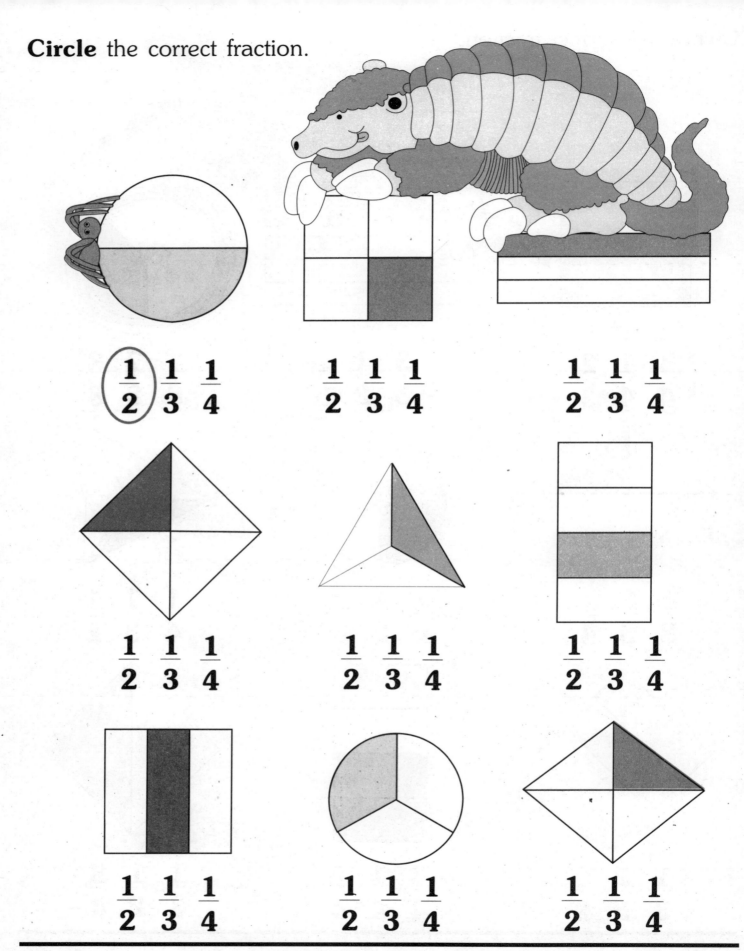

$\dfrac{1}{2}$ $\dfrac{1}{3}$ $\dfrac{1}{4}$

$\dfrac{1}{2}$ $\dfrac{1}{3}$ $\dfrac{1}{4}$

$\dfrac{1}{2}$ $\dfrac{1}{3}$ $\dfrac{1}{4}$

$\dfrac{1}{2}$ $\dfrac{1}{3}$ $\dfrac{1}{4}$

$\dfrac{1}{2}$ $\dfrac{1}{3}$ $\dfrac{1}{4}$

$\dfrac{1}{2}$ $\dfrac{1}{3}$ $\dfrac{1}{4}$

$\dfrac{1}{2}$ $\dfrac{1}{3}$ $\dfrac{1}{4}$

$\dfrac{1}{2}$ $\dfrac{1}{3}$ $\dfrac{1}{4}$

$\dfrac{1}{2}$ $\dfrac{1}{3}$ $\dfrac{1}{4}$

Chapter-1 What We Have Learnt

Page No 4

Count, write and then add.

(Left to right)

1+1=2   1+2=3   1+3=4
1+4=5   2+1=3   2+2=4
2+3=5   4+1=5

Page No 5

Find the sum.

(Downwards)

7   6   8   8

Page No 6

Count, write and then add.

(Downwards)

3+2=5   1+1=2   4+2=6

Page No 7

Count, write and then add.

(Downwards)

3+3=6   4+2=6   5+1=6

Page No 8

(Downwards)

Count, write and then add.

3+4=7   5+2=7   3+5=8

Page No 9

Add the units first and then add the tens.

(Across)

3.   46

6.   38

8.   57

10.   39

12.   79

14.   49

16.   28

19.   29

21.   36

23.   88

25.   49

(Down)

2.   93   4.   65

5.   43   7.   87

9.   79   11.   94

13.   92   15.   92

17.   83   18.   58

20.   94   24.   89

26.   98

Page No 10

Count, write and then subtract.

(Downwards)

4-2=2   5-3=2   6-4=2

113

Page No 11
(Downwards)
Count, write and then subtract.

6   6-1=5   6   6-4=2

5   5-3=2

Page No 12
Count, subtract and then write the remainder.
(Left to right)

2   4   4   2   3

Page No 13
Count, subtract and then write the remainder.
(Downwards)

8-3=5 5   7-2=5 5

7-5=2 2   7-5=2 2

Page No 14
Multiplication Tables: Revision
(Left to right)

42 21 12 0   81 64 90

16 14 24 40 25 42 16

18 0   30 30 36 60 9

100 56 ⌣

Page No 15
Multiply the following numbers.
(Downwards)

6   27 20 36 30 45

12 42 28 56

(Left to right)

36 81 50 80 15 20 32

36

Page No 16
Fill up the missing number.
(Left to right)

4 7 1 4 4 6 9

7 2 7 9 5 8 8

3 8

Page No 17
Now fill up the blanks.
(Left to right)

2 sets of 2=4   4 sets of 2=8

2+2=4   2+2+2+2=8

2x2=4   4x2=4

3 sets of 3=9   4 sets of 4=16

3+3+3=9   4+4+4+4=16

3x3=9   4x4=16

Page No 18
Now fill up the blanks.
(Left to right)

4x2=8   4x3=12 6x5=30

2x4=8   4x1=4   2x9=18

3x6=18 3x7=21

Page No 19
Now fill up the blanks.
(Left to right)

3x4=12 4x5=20   5x2=10

3x9=27 2x10=20   4x9=36

Page No 20
Fill up the blanks.
(Left to right)
4+4+4+4=16   5x3=15
9+9+9+9+9=45   6x6=36
3+3+3=9   2x8=16
7+7+7=21   4x7=28
7+7+7+7+7=35   5x9=45

Page No 21
Write the product.
(Downwards)
2   4   6   8   10   12
14   16   18   20
3   6   9   12   15   18
21   24   27   30
(Left to right)
8   8   18   18   12   12
14   14   6   6

Page No 22
Write the product.
(Downwards)
4   8   12   16   20   24
28   32   36   40
5   10   15   20   25   30
35   40   45   50
Draw sets.
(Left to right)

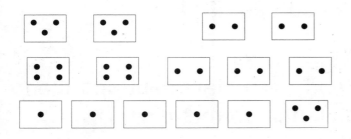

Page No 23
Write the product.
(Downwards)
6   12   18   24   30   36
42   48   54   60
7   14   21   28   35   42
49   56   63   70
Multiply as shown in the example below :
2x7=14   7x3=21
6x7=42   6x8=48
5x6=30   4x7=28
8x7=56

Page No 24
Write the product.
(Downwards)
8   16   24   32   40   48
56   64   72   80
9   18   27   36   45   54
63   72   81   90
Review
(Left to right)
16   21   32   45   28   15
24   54

Page No 25
Let's revise our multiplication tables first and then find the product.
(Left to right)
72   100   63   42   48   70
45   40   24   64   35   60
81   32   49   18   30   54
56   20   16   21   28   90
36   81   50

Page No 26
Read each set of numerals. Write them in order from the least to the greatest.
(Left to right)

10	12	15	36	45	49
19	25	81	18	24	36
29	41	57	30	55	72
26	56	66	72	78	87

Page No 27
(Left to right)
Read each set of numerals. Write them in order from the greatest to the least.

92	80	65	48	46	39
56	38	26	69	58	26
98	92	36	82	69	36
86	62	56	38	27	19

Page No 28
Read each number. Write how many tens and how many units there are.
(Left)

Tens	Units
4	3
2	8
3	0
5	4
6	5

(Right)

Tens	Units
1	7
7	1
6	6
1	9
8	1
4	0

Page No 29
Write the correct numeral.
(Left to right)

45	41	53	70	19
25	64	8	92	86
50	37	22		

Page No 32
(Left to right)
Look at each picture and write the correct numeral in each empty space.

Hundreds	Tens	Units
5	7	6
3	5	8
9	9	9
4	6	4
2	3	4
7	8	6

Page No 33
(Downwards)
Now read each numeral and then circle the correct answer.
280 800 512 180 966 324 678
700 555 90 944

Page No 34
Read each statement and then circle the correct digit.

(Downwards)

| 4 | 9 | 3 | 2 | 0 | 8 |
| 2 | 5 | 0 | 7 | 6 | 4 |

Peter's house number is   976.

Page No 35
Find the sum.
(Left to right)
800 750 621 400 918 900 834
910 862 600 700 820 897 850
835 800

Page No 36
Find the sum.
(Left to right)
892 682 690 795 994 593
893 651 871

Page No 37
Find the sum.
(Left to right)

995	1014	964
1185	1315	956
735	912	721
738	521	919
896	932	369
851		

Page No 38
Find the sum.
(Left to right)
198 267 886 246 451 117 362
264 532 172 775 375 595 485
481 683

Page No 39
Find the remainder.
(Left to right)
112 131 210 207 148
76   542 112 105 207
945 321 205 305 550
235

Page No 40
Find the remainder.
(Left to right)
124 801 412 321 350
330 61   504 458 431
207 623 723 117 148
412

Page No 41
Find the remainder.
(Left to right)
116 207 618 408 315
45   356 407 218

Page No 42
Find the sum or remainder.
(Left to right)
316 508 652 814 691
237 833 838 594 107
909 13   740 510 501
743 546 922

Page No 43
Put a cross (x) on each incorrect answer.

(Left to right)
97   496 98   342 496
35   329 86   325

Page No 44
Find the sum or remainder and circle the correct answer.
(Downwards)
491 939 201 736 828

Chapter-3.   Let's Read The Numerals
Page No 45
Now read and write the following numerals :

Hundreds	Tens	Units
4	0	0
1	6	9
2	0	8
2	8	4
8	8	3
9	1	2
7	3	4
2	5	0
1	8	8
9	9	9

Page No 46
Make numerals from the following.
560 952 702 613 860 111
999 899 600

Page No 47
Write in figures.
802 689 442 707 359 513
201
Write in words.
Seven hundred and eighty-five
Seven hundred and nine
Four hundred and nineteen
Nine hundred
Eight hundred and eighty-nine
Two hundred and eighty-six
Five hundred and seventy-one

Chapter-4. Before, After And Between
Page No 48
Fill up the box with the numeral that comes before the given numeral.
(Left to right)
308 472 499 998 137 386
644 866 911 259 764 343

Page No 49
Fill up the box with the numeral that comes after the given numeral.
860
249 Two hundred and forty-nine
744 Seven hundred and forty-four

665 Six hundred and sixty-five

370 Three hundred and seventy

900 Nine hundred

327 Three hundred and twenty-seven

906 Nine hundred and six

334 Three hundred and thirty-four

873 Eight hundred and seventy-three

Page No 50

Fill up the box with the numeral that comes between the given numerals.

(Left to right)

570 399 884 310 945 621

590 201 300 570 569 220

291 107 439 790 780 160

616 800

Chapter-5. Comparing Numbers

Page No 51

Now use one of the signs to compare the numbers below.

(Left to right)

> > < < < =

< < <

Put the numbers in order from the least to the greatest.

149 287 324 450 822

169 211 297 300 365

443 720 821 840 931

480 560 670 717 859

235 567 756 900 999

Page No 52

Place a > or < in each circle.

< (units) > (tens) > (units)

< (units) < (hundreds)

< (units) > (tens)

Put the numbers in order from the greatest to the least.

750 705 675 507

987 942 297 279

706 520 506 485

Chapter-6. Expanded Notation & Place Value

Page No 53

Write the following numbers in expanded notation using numerals.

500+60+2   900+50+3

300+70+5   600+10+7

100+00+9

Write the following numbers in expanded notation using words.

1 hundreds+ 0 tens + 9 units	Th	H	T	U
5 hundreds+ 1 tens+ 4 units	4	5	4	8
9 hundreds+ 3 tens + 6 units	3	6	5	3
3 hundreds+ 9 tens+ 8 units	1	4	8	9
6 hundreds+ 1 tens+ 7 units	6	1	3	6

Page No 54

Write each expanded notation in the form of a numeral.
884 627 465 759 248 531 392 156

Page No 55

Write the place value of each digit in each number. (Downwards)

793

7 hundreds   9 tens   3 units

436

4 hundreds   3 tens   6 units

Fill up the empty box. (Downwards)

1	10
200	2
50	500

Page No 58

Look at each picture and write the correct numeral in each empty space.

Page No 59

In each number below, one digit is in boldface. Circle the answer that shows the place value of that digit.

Units Hundreds Thousands
Thousands Tens   Units

Circle the correct digit.

1   4   2   7   5   7

Page No 60

Find the sum.

(Left to right)

5863	8385
5813	9022
9004	8106
6683	8852
7932	8113
7621	8173

Page No.61

Find the sum.

(Left to right)

961	1261	790
1243	4110	9911
5220	9910	8407

5573	8162	5976
4148	9457	4181
5188	4413	6841
8095	5337	

77	3897	309	485
891	2760	387	7452
5338	247	466	2148
1809	5999	857	4907
5717	989		

Page No 62
(Left to right)
Find the sum.

162	120	139
126	1007	1880
9672	9811	983
921	4676	9921

Page No 63
Find the remainder.
(Left to right)

2205	2736
4178	3089
1279	3144
713	1908

Page No 64
Find the remainder.
(Left to right)

87	379	271
6039	4722	4559
1651	3310	5112
1199	1600	6090
3089		

Page No.65
Find the remainder.
(Left to right)

Page No 66
Find the sum.
(Left to right)

7350	7160
9160	9210
1370	6000
3750	6023

Find the remainder.
(Left to right)

6690	2910	2580
7991	991	900
1327	2055	1124

Page No 67
Put a cross (x) on each incorrect answer.

3090	5417
7905	6390
6100	3100
1090	7124
8044	1568
7356	4427

Page No 68
Now read and write the following numerals.

121

Th	H	T	U
8	6	9	6
6	0	0	0
2	6	5	9
5	0	7	8
7	7	6	0
8	8	5	0
9	9	9	9
2	5	6	9
9	0	8	9
5	4	6	7

Page No 69

Make numerals from the following:

2072	9650	5432
4131	1987	6312
8935	3127	7671

Page No 70

Make numerals from the following:

5264	9274
6154	8734

Write in words

Eight thousand six hundred and forty-six

Nine thousand two hundred and twenty-one

Six thousand five hundred and twenty

Eight thousand seven hundred and forty-six

Chapter-9. Expanded Notation and Place value.

Page No 71

Break up the following numerals into thousands, hundreds, tens and units.

8000+200+70+5

1000+200+0+0

5000+600+80+0

9000+500+60+0

Write the numerals in expanded notation using words.

4 thousands+ 5 hundreds+ 8 tens + 2 units

1 thousands+ 0 hundreds+ 2 tens + 3 units

5 thousands+ 6 hundreds+ 8 tens + 0 units

7 thousands+ 8 hundreds+ 8 tens + 0 units

Page No 72

Write the correct digit in each blank.

Th	H	T	U
4	0	0	0
4	1	4	5
1	5	4	0

Write each numeral in its standard form.

7432	6341
2626	5893
8169	1095

Page No 73
(Across)

3. 397	5. 4780
7. 3333	8. 9035
9. 622	11. 678
13. 5390	15. 8126
16. 190	17. 2550

(Down)

2. 8433	3. 3036
4. 7392	6. 7354
10. 2599	11. 685
12. 822	14. 310

Page No 74
Write the place value of each digit in each number.

7000	900	30	7
4000	300	60	2
6000	400	30	2
5000	200	50	9
8000	600	90	7
9000	900	90	9

Page No 75
Write each set of numerals in order from the least to the greatest.

5	80	780	7937
4	56	460	2560
2	40	555	3257
8	50	670	3492
6	50	920	2080
9	22	920	4060

9   28   659   5069

Fill up the empty box.

9	90	900	9000
80	8	8000	800
600	6000	60	6
5000	500	5	50

Page No 78
Find the product.
(Left to right)

46	228	8664
46	906	9603
44	699	8888
66	848	8084
63	920	6428

Page No 79
Find the product
(Left to right)

906	2010	2046
364	1016	1578
1005	1920	2408

Page No 80
Find the product.
(Left to right)

1200	2500
5600	3600
1800	600
1600	2400
2000	1500
2800	7200

Page No 81
Find the product.
(Left to right)

2387	1012
5590	2332
1550	1475
2090	1001
1827	1125
240	1625
880	

Page No 82
Find the product.
(Left to right)

5733	8384
5368	5688
9718	15228
9660	55080
6678	17316
41082	47328

Page No 83
Find the product.
(Left to right)
180 568 171 232 300 232 609
285 75 675 396 444 186 370
472 168 224 220 228 504 644
294

Page No 84
Find each product in the number search below. Go horizontally and diagonally to search for each product.
(Left to right)

944	3900	938
2439	1152	270
1460	2016	

Page No 85
Write the division problems.

(Downwards)	(Downwards)
12÷3=4	8÷4=2
12÷4=3	8÷2=4
10÷2=5	18÷3=6
10÷5=2	18÷6=3
12÷6=2	20÷5=4
12÷2=6	20÷4=5

Page No 86
Divide the numbers. Write the quotient (answer).
(Left to right)
2   3   4   5   6   7

Page No 87
Divide the numbers. Write the quotient (answer).
(Left to right)
2   3   4   5   6   7

Page No 88
Divide the numbers. Write the quotient.

(Downwards)

2	2	2	3	4	5
6	7	8	9	9	5
9	4	5	3	4	7
3	3	8	6	7	8
16	9	3	10	4	9
2	6	7	10		

Page No 89

Write the division problem for each.

(Left to right)

36÷9=4 25÷5=5 42÷6=7

36÷4=9 25÷5=5 42÷7=6

24÷3=8 14÷2=7 35÷7=5

24÷8=3 14÷7=2 35÷5=7

72÷9=8 32÷8=4 45÷9=5

72÷8=9 32÷4=8 45÷5=9

36÷9=4 40÷8=5

36÷4=9 40÷5=8

Page No 90

Solve each of the following division problems. Write the multiplication problem that goes with the division problem.

4 4x9=36   9 9x6=54

3 3x3=9   4 4x7=28

4 4x10=40   8 8x11=88

7 7x12=84   5 5x3=15

9 9x12=108   6 6x10=60

8 8x4=32

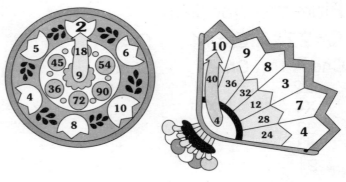

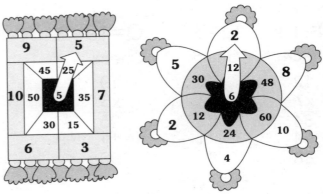

Page No 92

Find the quotient. (Each problem will have a remainder also.) Then check your answer.

(Left to right)

Q=9	Q=16	Q=7
Check	Check	Check
5	5	3
x 9	16	x7
45	80	21
+1	+1	+1
46	81	22

Q=8	Q=7
Check	Check
8	5
X8	X7
64	35
+7	+4
71	39

125

Page No 93
Find the quotient.

Q=22
Check
22
X4
───
88
+3
───
91

Q=14
Check
14
X6
───
84
+5
───
89

Q=25
Check
25
X3
───
75
+2
───
77

Q=12
Check
12
x7
───
84
+4
───
88

Q=31
Check
31
x2
───
62
+1
───
63

Q=19
Check
19
x5
───
95
+1
───
96

Page No 94
Find the quotient.
(Left to right)

Q=1303
Check
1303
x4
─────
5012
+0
─────
5012

Q=159
Check
159
x4
───
636
+2
───
638

Q=234
Check
236
x0
───
936
+0
───
936

Q=526
Check
526
x4
────
2104
+1
────
2105

Q=1213
Check
1213
x4
────
4852
+0
────
4852

Q=112
Check
112
x4
───
448
+1
───
449

Page No 95
Find the quotient.
(Left to right)

Q=17
Check
29
x17
────
493
+28
────
531

Q=69
Check
69
x30
────
2070
+0
────
2070

Q=31
Check
31
x30
────
930
+0
────
930

Q=144
Check
144
x43
────
6192
+8
────
6200

Q=8
Check
60
x8
────
480
+36
────
518

Q=29
Check
29
x21
────
609
+16
────
625

Page No 96
Find the quotient.
(Left to right)

Q=12	Q=8	Q=9
Q=8	Q=3	Q=12
Q=9	Q=4	Q=9
Q=7	Q=7	Q=12
Q=11	Q=4	Q=2
Q=9	Q=5	Q=11

Page No 97
Find the quotient.
(Left to right)

Q=19
Check
19
x2
───
38
+0
───
38

Q=31
Check
31
x6
───
186
+3
───
189

Q=13
Check
13
x7
───
91
+0
───
91

Q=41	Q=10	Q=17
Check	Check	Check

$$
\begin{array}{r} 41 \\ \times 5 \\ \hline 205 \\ +4 \\ \hline 209 \end{array}
\qquad
\begin{array}{r} 10 \\ \times 9 \\ \hline 90 \\ +5 \\ \hline 95 \end{array}
\qquad
\begin{array}{r} 17 \\ \times 3 \\ \hline 51 \\ +2 \\ \hline 53 \end{array}
$$

Q=12	Q=59	Q=83
Check	Check	Check

$$
\begin{array}{r} 12 \\ \times 6 \\ \hline 72 \\ +3 \\ \hline 75 \end{array}
\qquad
\begin{array}{r} 59 \\ \times 5 \\ \hline 295 \\ +3 \\ \hline 298 \end{array}
\qquad
\begin{array}{r} 83 \\ \times 6 \\ \hline 498 \\ +2 \\ \hline 500 \end{array}
$$

Chapter-12. Telling Time

Page No 98

Read the hour-hand first and then read the minute-hand. Write the time below each clock.

7 7:00   9 9:00   11 11:00

8 8:00   5 5:00

Page No 99

Read the hour-hand first and then read the minute-hand. Write the time below each clock.

4 4:30   10 10:30

6 6:30   8   8:30

12 12:30   3   3:30

Page No 100

Read the hour-hand first and

then read the minute-hand. Write the time below each clock.

8 8:15   1 1:15

12 12:15   10 10:15

7 7:15

Page No 101

Read the hour-hand first and then read the minute-hand. Write the time below each clock.

9 8:45   1 12:45   7 6:45

2 1:45   10 9:45

Page No 102

Write the minutes on each line.

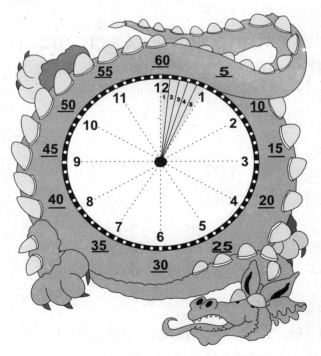

There are 60 minutes in an hour.

Page No 103

Write the amount on the line.

8   15   7

Page No 104
What is the price of each toy?
Count the coins below. Write
the amount on the line.

5 10 15 20 25 26 27
5 10 15 17 19 20
5 7 9 10 11 12
5 10 12 14 15

Page No 105
Write the amount on each
line.
Is there enough money to pay
for each item ?

17 No 14 No
13 Yes 17 No

Page No 106
Count the coins in each group
Write the amount on the line.
(Left to right)
17 10 15 14 19

Page No 107
(Left to right)

44	44	36	36	17
+45	+17	+39	+45	+28
89	61	75	81	45

Page No 108
Write the correct fraction for
each shaded object.
(Left to right)
2 3 1
4 1 1

Page No 109
Colour the shape. Write the
fraction for each shape.
(Left to right)

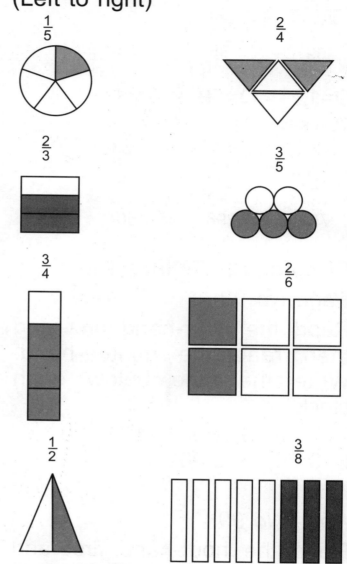

$\frac{1}{5}$ $\frac{2}{4}$

$\frac{2}{3}$ $\frac{3}{5}$

$\frac{3}{4}$ $\frac{2}{6}$

$\frac{1}{2}$ $\frac{3}{8}$

Page No 111
Circle the correct fraction.
(Left to right)

$\frac{1}{3}$ $\frac{3}{8}$ $\frac{1}{4}$ $\frac{2}{6}$ $\frac{1}{3}$ $\frac{2}{3}$ $\frac{2}{4}$ $\frac{1}{2}$

Page No 112
Circle the correct fraction.
(Left to right)

$\frac{1}{2}$ $\frac{1}{4}$ $\frac{1}{3}$ $\frac{1}{4}$ $\frac{1}{3}$ $\frac{1}{4}$ $\frac{1}{3}$ $\frac{1}{3}$ $\frac{1}{4}$